Glasnost—
Soviet Cinema Responds

T0338848

Texas Film Studies Series
Thomas Schatz, Editor

Glasnost—
Soviet Cinema
Responds

By **NICHOLAS GALICHENKO**

Edited by ROBERT ALLINGTON

University of Texas Press, Austin

Copyright © 1991 by the University of Texas Press
All rights reserved
Printed in the United States of America

First Edition, 1991

Requests for permission to reproduce material from this work should be
sent to Permissions, University of Texas Press, Box 7819, Austin, Texas
78713-7819.

ⓧ The paper used in this publication meets the minimum requirements of
American National Standard for Information Sciences—Permanence of
Paper for Printed Library Materials, ANSI Z39.48-1984.

For reasons of economy and speed this volume has been printed from camera-ready copy furnished by the author, who assumes full responsibility for
its contents.

Library of Congress Cataloging-in-Publication Data

Galichenko, Nicholas, 1943–
   Glasnost—Soviet cinema responds / by Nicholas Galichenko ; edited by
Robert Allington. — 1st ed.
      p.   cm. — (Texas film studies series)
   Includes bibliographical references and index.
   ISBN 978-0-292-72753-3
      1. Motion pictures—Soviet Union.   2. Motion picture producers and
directors—Soviet Union.   I. Allington, Robert, 1945–
   II. Title.   III. Series.
   PN1993.5.R9G35   1991
   791.43'0947—dc20   91-580
                                                                      CIP

Contents

Illustrations

Listed by film title or subject, in order of appearance

Preface:
Recent Soviet Film
—One Critic's Choice

Glasnost—*Soviet Cinema Responds* is the result of many hours in darkened theaters making notes to the glow of a penlight, of numerous interviews with Soviet directors, actors, actresses, and film industry officials, and of my personal observations made during a trip to the Soviet Union in 1987 for the 15th International Film Festival in Moscow.

The Soviet film industry produces some 130 feature length movies in an average year. In addition to this, the recent outpouring of works, delayed by censors, held in cold storage in the pre-glasnost era and now released, makes the choice of directors and film works to be included in a text such as this an onerous task.

The text is structured as a series of three essays, and a filmography of the directors of the glasnost cinema. Throughout the book, still photographs and reproductions of Soviet poster art help to illustrate the work. These images have been reproduced through the courtesy of Sovexportfilm.

The first essay, "The Age of Perestroika," outlines the changes that have occurred in the cinema of the U.S.S.R., provides some historical observations on the socialist realist tradition and the legacy of Stalinism, and takes a look at the influential film educator and director Mikhail Romm, whose students are now transforming the Soviet motion picture medium. The second, "Youth in Turmoil," is a somewhat sociological view of films about youth—the most dynamic and socially revealing of present productions. The third, "Odysseys in Inner Space," examines the new direction in Soviet Cinema as a focus on the inner world of individuals—a journey of philosophical dimension that brings East and West closer in their perceptions and their values.

The filmography is a guide to the works of some of the most significant contemporary Soviet directors and to the effects that glasnost and perestroika have had on their lives and their art. This section is intended to complement the essays and to provide a guide for interested researchers. (Many of the films discussed herein have had their original, Russian titles rendered into English in several semantically different ways upon translation. Thus a single Soviet film may be released in the West under several different titles. To aid in the identification of these films for our readers who may not speak Russian, the filmography contains a listing of all the alternate titles – in English – for a particular film. Where this confusing situation has arisen, the various titles will be listed together, separated by a typed slash; the title which enjoys the greatest currency will be listed first.) Our approach, while giving a comprehensive listing of all a director's films, is selective in its discursive intent—abbreviated discussions center around the contemporary cultural transition.

I would like to thank my editor, Robert Allington, of the Creative Writing Department at the University of Victoria, who collaborated with me from the book's inception, suggested stylistic and research approaches, honed the text, and brought the manuscript to camera-ready copy. What we have attempted to do here is record a social revolution, not as it has affected the discussions in the Party conferences of the U.S.S.R. or the international arena, but as it has changed the aesthetic form of cinema.

I am also indebted to Louis Menashe, professor of Russian History and PBS television producer, and to David Paul, East European cinema scholar and critic, who read the text prior to production and provided helpful commentary.

Some years ago when I attended a film workshop at the Center for Soviet and East European Studies at the University of Illinois, Professor Ludmila Pruner, an expert on the work of Andrei Tarkovsky and a wonderfully informed specialist on cinema in the U.S.S.R., inspired in me an interest in contemporary Soviet film. It was from her that I first learned of the marvelous works of such film directors as Kira Muratova and others who subsequently gained prominence in the Age of Perestroika. If *Glasnost—Soviet Cinema Responds* can inspire others as Professor Pruner did me, I shall be most gratified.

N. V. Galichenko,

Glasnost—
Soviet Cinema Responds

1 • *The Age Of Perestroika*

Avel Aravidze is having nightmares. He wakes up choking. His son, Tornike, asks too many questions. Avel's father, Varlam, was an important man, the mayor of the town, the Party boss. The things he did, he did for the common cause. How can Tornike, the pure soul, understand how it was then, in the '30s, in the time of the Great Terror?

Varlam is dead but he won't stay buried.

Three times the old man's body has been dug up. Three times it has appeared in the family garden. What has he done that someone will not let him rest in peace? A neighbor, Ketevan Barateli is arrested and charged as a graverobber. Her trial begins and the horror unveils itself. Varlam has caused the deaths of thousands, among them Ketevan's father, an artist who objected to a church being turned into a science center.

"What are you?" Tornike demands. "What have you lived for?"

Cynically, Avel condones Varlam's sins. Tornike commits suicide. Avel in despair digs up Varlam's corpse again and casts it over a precipice. Repenting, he sends the beast to the pit with a curse:

"Damn you, Satan," he says.

The Aravidzes and Ketevan Barateli are characters in Tengiz Abuladze's *Repentance*, a two and a half hour film epic produced at the Gruziafilm Studio in the Soviet Republic of Georgia. The film is the standard-bearer of a cultural revolution. That revolution is *glasnost,* the Russian term which in the West is synonymous with the reform program of Premier Mikhail Gorbachev. Glasnost, like our ideal of Free Speech, is an abstract notion. It achieves its true significance only in social context. Literally it consists of two syllables: *glas* (voice) and *nost* (quality or condition). Voiceness, if you like. The closest word in English is probably "outspokenness," or "publicity," although the most common translation in the popular media has been "openness."

In the cinema, glasnost can be measured by the films released since Gorbachev's rise to power, by the perceptions of the artists who make the films and by the responses of the Soviet people who have seen them. In this respect, glasnost for the film industry has been very much a retrospective phenomenon. Many films which may be associated with the glasnost era were made prior to Gorbachev's liberalizing reforms, but were suppressed by the policies of his predecessors, and never seen by the public. Released at last for distribution, these works may truly be considered films of the glasnost era, as they share with other, more current works the unifying characteristic of a truth that could not be told until now.

The glasnost movies are eye openers: Stalinist persecution, Jewish emigration, social alienation, even police brutality come under the scrutiny of the lens. The didactic, pompous works of the past are gone. Science fantasy, docudrama, political satire, and such long-buried subjects as human spirituality are now actively explored.

The artists took to glasnost with a radical fervor. The Soviet Filmmakers Union (SFU) in a secret-ballot election chose the frequently banned and often out-of-favor Elem Klimov as its first secretary. Klimov, in his two-year term, was instrumental in freeing dozens of suppressed works and was responsible for implementing reforms which have virtually ended post and pre-production censorship. Audiences may now watch Andrei Konchalovsky's *Asya's Happiness*, which had been frozen since 1966; Klimov's 1964 satire of party politics, *Welcome, But No Unauthorized Admission*; and the entire works of the cinematic genius Andrei Tarkovsky, who like Konchalovsky left the U.S.S.R. for work in the West.

The people have been loving it. For them it's a chance to reclaim some of their personal and national history. Abuladze's *Repentance*, which was delayed four years by pre-glasnost censors, subsequently played to packed theaters, and over 1,000 prints were placed in circulation. Releases such as Yuri Podnieks' anti-Afghan-war documentary *Is It Easy to Be Young?* had young people lining up for hours to see themselves on the screen.

Repentance is a surreal religious allegory with its roots in Georgia's ancient and modern history. This was the Caucasian nation which gave birth to Joseph Stalin. Neither Stalin nor his feared henchman Lavrenti Beria is directly mentioned in the film, but the allusions are unmistakable. The tyrant Varlam is a black-clad figure who wears Beria-style pince-nez. After the 22nd Party Congress in 1961, in response to Nikita Khrushchev's denunciation of Stalinism, the dictator's remains were removed from the Lenin mausoleum and interred instead beneath the Kremlin wall. Only in Georgia does his statue still stand. In ancient times Georgia was a part of another realm. The dominant state was Rome, and the apostles of Christianity were evangelizing it. Georgia and her sister state Armenia were the first areas within the modern boundaries of the U.S.S.R. to adopt the faith. In *Repentance* that heritage reemerges. Like Bergman's *The Seventh Seal*, it evokes the images of the *Revelations of St. John the Divine* and other portions of the Christian scriptures, to weave its apocalyptic message. At Ketevan's trial, in a curious scene reminiscent of Paul's defense before Festus and Agrippa, soldiers in armor stand at attention and the woman announces:

"You may bury him (Varlam) seven by seven times and I will dig him up seven by seven times. Such a man isn't worthy of resting peacefully in his native earth."

In the *Acts of the Apostles*, Festus thinks Paul mad. In *Repentance*, Avel seeks to have Ketevan sent to an asylum. Paul declares his witness: "That they should repent and do works meet for repentance." Neither Agrippa nor the magistrates of the Georgian court can find their defendants guilty.

Ketevan sets herself against the sins of Stalinism embodied in Varlam, much as *Revelations* condemns the Doctrine of Balaam which forced the children of Israel into idolatry. Ketevan's father is sentenced to hard labor in a lumber camp. She and her mother join others who wait anxiously for news from the prisoners, which arrives periodically etched on logs at the railway station. She never sees her father again. He has been "transferred, no address." His name in the language of *Revelations* is still written in the Book of Life.

"Just tell me he's dead. Tell me he's dead," wails a demented woman in another scene.

In the 1980s, mothers and lovers waited for the body bags and the wounded veterans to come back from Afghanistan. In Podnieks' *Is It Easy to Be Young?*, a mother talks of trembling at the sight of the postal carrier. Her son returns with a badly damaged limb. At first he loses himself in drink daily, but when the leg heals he goes to work as a firefighter, because there he finds the familiar extremes of war. The film is a group portrait of the '80s generation. It begins at an outdoor rock concert in Riga. Teenagers with upraised arms bounce in mass passion to the power of the music and the militia move in to quell their enthusiasm. On the train leaving the amphitheater they run amok and destroy two railway cars. About 100 people are involved, but one young man gets three years in prison as a result. In a poignant court scene he asks if he is more to blame than his cohorts. Another youth is shown at the morgue tearing bodies apart.

"It doesn't matter to me what I chop up," he says.

The works that have emerged to date from the glasnost cinema are

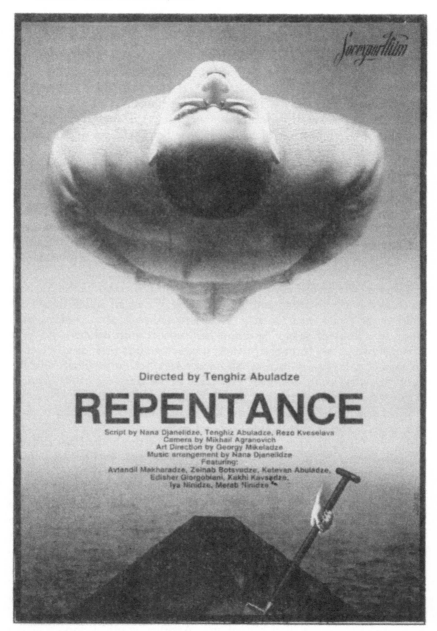

REPENTANCE: "You may bury him seven by seven times and I will dig him up seven by seven times," says *Repentance* heroine Ketevan Barateli, speaking of the tyrant Varlam. (Poster Art: Courtesy Sovexportfilm)

almost universally gray. They show a society in some senses more affluent and more stable than its heritage of revolution, political purges
and the Great Patriotic War, but at the same time a culture in search of
meaning, questioning its heavy-handed institutions and looking for a
path out of the alienation of the modern state. The heroic models of the
revolution did not fit the real world of the '80s. The bloody history of
Stalinism had to be shown if only to purge its ghost. The bright
promises of the Khrushchev era now seem hollow and the youth born
of that generation find themselves in turmoil, misunderstood, in despair
of growing up. The adult relationships portrayed on the screen are also
not pretty ones—divorce, loneliness, men and women looking for some
purpose, some way to define their roles. The cinema artists' views of the
future are no better. In Konstantin Lopushansky's *Letters from a Dead
Man*, produced by the Lenfilm Studio, the world has collapsed following a nuclear disaster. In Georgi Danelia's satirical *Kin-Dza-Dza*, from
the Mosfilm Studio, the mores of the black marketeers have triumphed
and a new social order based on their principles is in place.

Although the cinematic images are not hopeful, the fact that they
have been shown presents a glimmer of optimism. Underlying the heavy
messages, too, there is often a wry sense of humor.

When I interviewed Rezo Kveselava, a scriptwriter for *Repentance*,
he quoted Albert Schweitzer.

"Today's pessimists are optimists," he said. "And the optimists are
pessimists."[1]

Purging Stalin's Ghost From The Film Industry

In Yevgeni Yevtushenko's poem "The Heirs of Stalin," the
poet watches as the pipe-smoking despot's coffin is moved. Thin smoke
curls from the casket and breath seems to escape through the chinks.
Grimly clenching his embalmed fists, he is only pretending to be dead.

"You may bear Stalin out of the Mausoleum," says Yevtushenko.
"But how, out of Stalin, shall we bear Stalin's heirs?"[2]

The period 1956 to 1965 in the U.S.S.R. was a time of liberalization
in the literary arts, known as the Thaw. It was signalled by Ilya Ehrenburg's 1954 novel of the same name. New fiction and poetry came to
prominence then, partly because it suited Khrushchev's de-Stalinization
policies and partly because there was an underground press network,
samizdat, which circulated controversial works by avant-garde writers.
There was no equivalent of samizdat in the cinema. The cost of production and the means of distribution made that impossible. The cinema,
more susceptible to censorship and state control, was more conservative;

in its bureaucracy the heirs of Stalin still ruled. Gorbachev has changed that.

What glasnost is for the Soviet film industry is in effect a new theory of state aesthetics. Western leaders, even a movie star president of the U.S.A., are not expected to make pronouncements on such matters, but in the U.S.S.R. it is a tradition.

The so-called "Lenin Proportions," a term derived from Lenin's directions for the use of literature and cinema as tools in the cultural revolution,[3] guided what was seen in Soviet motion picture theaters in the 1920s. In 1957, as a part of governmental rapprochement with the artistic community, *For a Close Link Between Literature and Art and the Life of the People*, a collection of three speeches by Nikita Khrushchev to a writers' conference held at the headquarters of the Central Committee of the CPSU (Communist Party of the Soviet Union), was published in the Soviet magazine *Kommunist.*

Gorbachev's glasnost is of course more than just a new aesthetic. It is a broadly based social policy that includes economic, political and ideological components. It has called for *perestroika* (a restructuring of the economy and workplace), *democratizatsia* (democratization of the party and elections for previously appointed positions) and *samouprav-lenie* (self-management). Each of these elements has had its effect on the film industry, but for writers and directors the most important is *novoye myshlenie* (new thinking). For the intelligentsia, what *novoye myshlenie* amounts to is a change in methodology—issues should be approached by asking frank questions rather than seeking dogmatic answers. The handmaiden of the new thinking is *novaya publicistika* (the new journalism).

Perestroika brought revolutionary change to the Soviet motion picture industry. The Congress of Soviet Cinematographers, in 1986, saw an immediate and enthusiastic response to the liberalizations announced by Party Chairman Mikhail Gorbachev at the 27th Congress of the Communist Party of the Soviet Union. Shortly after the policy was announced, Filip Yermash, the long-entrenched president of Goskino (the State Film Board) was bounced. The reform-minded Alexander Kamshalov took the helm. Kamshalov cut Goskino red tape, abandoned the film board's unilateral control over censorship and gave the studios both creative and financial autonomy: in effect, a new model.

Goskino for decades was dominated by an old guard whose opinions had their genesis in the socialist realist aesthetic of the Stalinist era. The artist in this tradition is "an engineer of human souls" whose function in representing reality is guided by three tenets: *ideinost* (ideological purity), *partiinost* (party-mindedness) and *narodnost* (mass consciousness). Art was thus contained by its higher purpose: the ideological

LETTERS FROM A DEAD MAN: In Lopushansky's science fiction film *Letters from a Dead Man* the world has collapsed following a nuclear disaster. (Photo: Courtesy Sovexportfilm)

transformation of the viewer. Khrushchev, despite his initial support of the Thaw, never quite managed to transcend these classical precepts.

"The highest destiny of art and literature is to mobilize the people to the struggle for new advances in the building of Communism," he wrote in his *For a Close Link Between Literature and Art and the Life of the People.* [4]

"For the artist," he said, "the question of whether he is free or not does not arise. For him the question of which approach to the phenomena of reality to choose is clear. He need not conform or force himself; the true representation of life from the point of view of Communist *partiinost* is a necessity of his soul."

The necessities of soul for the artists whose films have been released in the Age of Perestroika appear to have a different foundation. In Lopushansky's *Letters from a Dead Man*, a scientist who is expiring from radiation poisoning addresses his colleagues for the last time:

"Man continued to love and love created Art. Art which depicted our otherworldly longing, the howl of lonely thinking beings in the frigid cosmic wasteland."

The scientist has been responsible for the innovations that led to the nuclear holocaust. As his speech ends, he kneels down to pray.

"Jesus forgive me," he says.

Glasnost, like free speech, carries with it the connotation of accountability. There have been other periods of glasnost in Russian history, but each of them has ended with increased repression. In the 18th century, glasnost was linked to Peter the Great's rationalization of the state bureaucracy. In the 19th century, the term was the buzzword of the so-called "enlightened bureaucrats" of the time. Its function was not to challenge the forces of the state, but to consolidate autocratic authority. By reducing the radical pressures that come from the suppression of ideas, it was meant to generate middle-of-the-road public opinion which would ultimately ensure the survival of the Czar. The policy helped to bring about the emancipation of serfs, but it also created other unrealized reformist expectations.

The Thaw of the Khrushchev administration soon offended its sponsor. It fostered a new spirit of national idealism expressed in the poetry of Yevgeni Yevtushenko and Andrei Voznesensky, but it also produced Alexander Solzhenitsyn. Khrushchev could not control the illicit distribution of literature by samizdat, but the movies were more manageable. The filmmakers who failed to conform to his traditional views of art were soon brought in check. When Marlen Khutsiev's 1963 film drama *I'm Twenty* displeased the premier, he launched an immediate attack on it. The film was seen as formalist, avant-garde, and unflattering to the state officials. As a result, it was severely edited. *I'm Twenty* is

FAREWELL: In Elem Klimov's *Farewell* a primitive ancestral culture is threatened by the construction of a hydro-electric project. The film was banned by pre-glasnost censors. (Poster: Courtesy Sovexportfilm)

one of the films that under the new leadership is again available in its original uncut version.

The Thaw lasted from 1956 to shortly after Khrushchev's fall from power in 1964. Despite its limitations, one cannot underestimate the importance of the Kremlin's temporary reconciliation with the intelligentsia. It was during this period that the Moscow Film School (VGIK) admitted some of the most innovative figures in Soviet cinema: Tarkovsky, Panfilov, Konchalovsky, Mikhalkov, Klimov and others. By 1962, Khrushchev and his party leaders were questioning the wisdom of their policies. Under Brezhnev, the Thaw turned to an icy chill. Many major works were banned. Alexei Gherman's *My Friend Ivan Lapshin*, Panfilov's *Theme* and Klimov's *Farewell* all went into deep freeze.

Writers and artists of the Post-Thaw period turned to the safe themes of the village prose school, a genre which idealizes the life of simple country people. Village prose, as long as it made no mention of the intelligentsia and scrupulously avoided controversy, was permitted. Films such as *My Friend Ivan Lapshin, Theme*, and *Farewell* broke the rules. All of them had provincial settings, but Gherman presented a far-from-idyllic view of a policeman, Panfilov examined the lot of the writer too realistically for comfort, and Klimov portrayed an historic Russian village destroyed by a state water diversion project.

Farewell is based on Valentin Rasputin's novella *Farewell to Matyora*. It is one of the ironies of the Post-Thaw period that Rasputin's work could be read, but it could not be seen on the screen. Matyora is a fictional island in Siberia. The construction of a hydro-electric power station necessitates the relocation of villagers who live, as they have for centuries, close to the earth. The worship of trees still survives here. The veneration of the land and its life-forms frames the consciousness of the people. For Darya Pinegin it was the place of her birth. She became a bride, she worked, she raised children, she grew old among Matyora's familiar edifices—the churches, the farms, and the homes, many of which were there before her and which she thinks should remain after her.

Early in the film we see Darya alone in the forest. In a magical copse she intones a primitive chant to Mother Earth—the blessed ground from which all life and beauty come. As the flooding begins, she stays behind to protest the destruction. In solemn supplication she sanctifies her home, casting out belongings, scrubbing the walls in exhausting labor and then closing the shutters before offering it up to the flood. She and other villagers huddle together to await their fate. The authorities try desperately to reach them; but fog, a symbol of blind official policy, sets in and they are lost.

Mikhail Gorbachev has read Rasputin's novels, has seen the Klimov film and was apparently moved by it. Among his political initiatives is a plan for the restoration and resettlement of ancestral hamlets. At the Denver International Film Festival in October 1986, Klimov mentioned his personal discussions with the premier:

"I found out he loves films," Klimov said. [5]

Unfortunately for earlier Soviet filmmakers, the same could be said of Joseph Stalin.

The Romm Connection

*T*he individualist director Mikhail Romm made his first film under Stalin. His last picture was completed in the Brezhnev era. Romm was perhaps VGIK's most influential film educator since the school was founded by Lev Kuleshov in 1919. He was certainly as inspirational a figure to the young post-Stalinist cinematographers as Kuleshov was to the experimentalists in the 1920s. To look at a list of the 1987 members of the Soviet Filmmakers Union (SFU) secretariat is to look at the names of Romm's proteges. Elem Klimov, the first secretary, Sergei Soloviev of the young directors committee, Gleb Panfilov of the fiction committee and Grigori Chukhrai of the legal committee were all Romm's students. The list does not end here. Vasili Shukshin and Andrei Tarkovsky (both deceased), Andrei Konchalovsky, Georgi Danelia, Tengiz Abuladze, Nikita Mikhalkov and Vadim Abrashitov all studied with Romm.

Romm admired the non-conformist, the eccentric, the independent thinker. In almost every instance, the candidates he selected for admission to VGIK were those whom other examiners would have refused to admit. The anecdotes about Romm's intuitive approach to seeking out talent are still told in the halls of VGIK.

When Sergei Soloviev applied to the school, it is said, he was accused of plagiarism. The admissions committee refused to take his oral examination. The brilliantly conceived script he wrote could not be his own, they said.

"Prove it," said Mikhail Romm.

One examiner said the work was a Paustovsky story. Another claimed it was Bunin and yet another, Prishvin. Romm sent them to the library to substantiate their claims. The case could not be proved. When Soloviev appeared before them, Romm conducted the questioning.

> ***Romm:*** Have you read any books?
> ***Soloviev:*** Yes.
> ***Romm:*** Do you have any favorites?

Soloviev: Yes.
Romm: Do you want to be a film director?
Soloviev: Yes.
Romm: See, he answered all the questions correctly. I give him full marks.

The story about Soloviev's interview is typical. Tarkovsky, who was from a well-known artistic family and already established in the arts, arrived for his oral examination behaving like a fop. His patrician air and his condescending attitude were not well received, but Romm urged his acceptance. Vasili Shukshin came looking like a muzhik. A Siberian peasant who had only a few years of formal education yet was the headmaster of a village school, Shukshin shocked examiners when he revealed his ignorance of Tolstoy.

"Have you ever heard of Nikolai Nekrasov?" they asked Shukshin.

He exploded angrily at the question about the 19th-century poet who wrote on peasant themes.

"I had a few drinks with him," he said. "He was a personal acquaintance."

Romm convinced the committee to take Shukshin because he was impressed with the man's nerve.

Each of Romm's students carries on his vision. Soloviev was recently the SFU-supported candidate for the dean's position at VGIK. The thrust for *democratizatsia* there pitted him against the Goskino candidate, Alexander Novikov. The appointment of Novikov, the former assistant dean who has a doctoral degree, was eventually confirmed by the Minister of Education, but not without a verbal and impassioned protest from students who thought an election should be held.

Grigori Chukhrai, like his mentor, headed up the Mosfilm Experimental Studio. He also founded its television counterpart ETO, the Department of Experimental Television. Soloviev is today as popular a teacher as Romm once was. And Elem Klimov has been busy changing the direction of the entire industry.

Rolan Bykov, the youth committee chairman of SFU, has said of Romm's influence: "Those who wished to be directors had to go to Romm." Bykov worked at Romm's Mosfilm workshop, the studio which was the training ground of many of today's leading directors.

None of Romm's former students, however, has had more effect on the contemporary structure of the film industry than Elem Klimov. Klimov, during his tenure as SFU first secretary, and Alexander Kamshalov, the new Goskino head, established the policy that the first secretary and the Goskino president would co-sign all documents concerning the film industry. A conflict committee of SFU, created by

Klimov, would mediate when the release of films was in dispute and the union would even have a voice in deciding which foreign films the Soviet public sees. SFU delegates sit on the Goskino buying committee. The committee has representatives from both Sovexportfilm (the industry marketing agency) and from the union, but more than half the delegates are members of the SFU secretariat.

Klimov and Kamshalov as a team became the co-architects of perestroika for the motion picture industry. Under Kamshalov's direction the state film board has undergone major structural and administrative modification. The new Goskino functions primarily as a co-ordinating and distribution center. Under the former old-guard board every script had to be submitted for official sanction. Now only the subject matter has to be approved. Goskino retains creative control only with foreign co-productions and films which require specialized equipment. The major studios are expected to be self-supporting and self-managed, although smaller republican studios will receive supplementary grants to ensure their survival. Goskino also assumes some of the risk of first pictures by new directors and offers incentives for the production of science fiction, musical and youth films.

All this is a quantum leap from the bureaucratic, socialist-realist environment of the old board. In the past, science fiction was only marginally exploited in the cinema. The musical too has not been a significant genre. Science fiction, as the Art of Cognitive Wonder, is experimentalist. It journeys to new worlds—fantastic futures which challenge reality. Dogma is anathema to it. It seeks the truth free from the limits of time and space. Music is a primal art—non-rational, dionysian. In its emotive force, it is boundless. Both genres resist the fetters of ideological constraint.

Retro-film perspectives in the musical were acceptable in the socialist-realist tradition, but were often subject to protracted criticism. Music of the contemporary artistic subculture was assigned to basements rather than the silver screen. Scientific realism was welcome, but science fantasy was suspect.

Grigori Alexandrov's *Jolly Fellows (Jazz Comedy)* arrived on the scene in 1934, the landmark year when the Soviet Writers' Congress first inscribed in stone the canons of socialist realism. The film was a comedic retrospective of the NEP period.[*] It was taken to task as "lacking

---

[*] NEP Period (1921-27). Deriving both its name and its character from Lenin's New Economic Policy, which relaxed state control of the economy, the NEP Period was a time of economic and intellectual relaxation, and experimentation in the arts. It was concurrent with the Golden Age of Soviet Cinema, which produced Eisenstein, Vertov, Dovzhenko and Pudovkin.

socialist backbone." The socialist-realist hero was larger-than-life, neo-classical in dimension, the ideal man, without doubts, with few faults. *Jolly Fellows*, as a musical comedy, required a flawed hero, someone whose imperfections made him laughable. The film's only saving grace was that it poked fun at an epoch that was in disrepute. The musicals of glasnost present a sharp contrast to those of the retro-film genre. Pictures, such as Soloviev's *ASSA*, discussed in Chapter 2, take a solid look at today's rock music culture and treat that music as a serious art form.

Lenin's social policy, like Gorbachev's glasnost, was a reflection of the socio-political realities of his time. NEP was Lenin's admission that the post-revolutionary economy was not working. Social and artistic freedom provided hope. The Stalinist era was marked by forced collectivization, industrialization and the Great Patriotic War (World War II). The positive hero suited it. The Stakhanovite* labor ethic was the ideal. With glasnost, a mature world power responds to a populace which is more concerned with quality of life than with abstract ideological goals. The frontiers that remain to be conquered are those of social development. Gorbachev in the midst of the Afghan war called for a restructuring of domestic life, much as Lyndon Johnson announced the Great Society while conflict raged in Vietnam.

The scientific realism that was encouraged under the socialist-realist doctrine was also a product of its time. When Mikhail Romm's 1962 film *Nine Days of One Year* was produced, Yuri Gagarin had just become the first human in space. In science, it was believed, lay the hope for the future. That kind of faith in science is not possible for artists today. Chernobyl has put an end to it. The hero of *Nine Days of One Year* is Dmitri Gusev, a dedicated nuclear physicist who is ultimately willing to die for his work. Such a hero has the attributes of the classical socialist-realist protagonist, but to view Romm as conforming entirely to the conventional aesthetic would be a mistake. Romm was an innovator as well as a survivor. His hero's pursuit of scientific and social advancement is futile. It consumes him in workaholism. It destroys his marriage. He continues to experiment with nuclear energy despite the fact that he has already absorbed two doses of radiation and knows that the third will kill him. The contrast of ideas rather than the action creates the drama in the film. Narrative form is set aside. The director focuses on nine days in Gusev's life impinging on nine parts of one year in which Gusev, his unhappy wife and his skeptical co-worker debate the merits of life versus the quest for truth. Romm's fascination was

---

*   Stakhanov, a cult figure, the man who produced more coal than any other miner. He was the role model that others were expected to emulate.

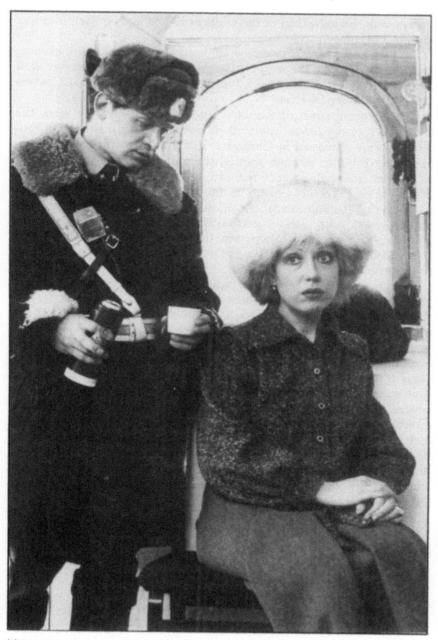

THEME: In Gleb Panfilov's *Theme* almost everyone is a writer. Here poet/traffic-cop Yuri commiserates with biographer/museum guide Sasha. (Photo: Courtesy Sovexportfilm)

always with the individual in the midst of the collective. Each film was for him a personal quest.

"A film, any film, is a director's confession, an expression of his outlook on the events in the world. If he repeats himself in anyway at all, it means he has turned into a hack," he wrote in his film manual *Conversations about Film Directing.* [6]

The preoccupation of Romm's student Gleb Panfilov with the individual's search for artistic truth is not unlike his master's. In Panfilov's *Theme*, discussed in Chapter 3, a successful writer, Kim Yesenin, has betrayed his art through political compromise. His accommodations bring him financial rewards but little peace. He leaves his wife and friends behind. Yesenin retreats to the sacred precinct of Russian Orthodoxy, the Vladimir-Suzdal region, to start work on a new play. There he encounters other literary personalities: a dissident who works as a gravedigger, a poet/traffic-cop, and the stunningly beautiful museum guide, Sasha. who is also working on a book. The dissident, a Jew, wants to emigrate.

"Death is living in a country where one cannot practice the craft which gives one Life," the dissident says.

Through painful introspection, through contact with others, and his relationship with Sasha, Yesenin experiences an inner rebirth. Such a restoration of the spirit, a *samoperestroika,** was essential to artistic creation, in the view of Mikhail Romm. Prior to the production of *Nine Days of One Year*, Romm went seven years without making a movie. This was the period immediately following Stalin's death, an era of noncinema when almost no films were made. Romm was one of the few directors who was offered contracts, but he refused them.

It was for him a time of personal catharsis. He spent his waking hours making speeches, denouncing the personality cult, proclaiming his debt to those who had been executed, decrying the bankruptcy of artists who inwardly were still locked in the Stalinist psychology. He was at the apex of his career, yet until he spoke out, he could not work again.

"It is important to recognize what there is of your own in yourself and that which is someone else's," Romm wrote in *Conversations about Film Directing*. "First I must shed the skin of habit before making another film. With years, a person becomes more clever, but in the selection of his impressions—what he sees, what he hears—there is the influence of his profession and of convention. This is bad." [7]

The reformer Klimov brought *samoperestroika* to the Soviet Filmmakers Union. The Writers Congress of 1934 sought macrorevolution, the "engineering of human souls," of external society, through

---

* Samoperestroika, a restructuring of oneself.

ideologically correct art. Klimov's manifesto, "The Reconstruction of the Filmmaker," seeks a microrevolution: to change society, first the filmmakers must change themselves.

"Our union began decisive activity in bringing back to health our film industry in the Year of the Tiger," Klimov told the second plenary session of SFU early in 1987. "Now we are entering the Year of the Rabbit. From our common everyday understanding, the rabbit is a simple-hearted, timid creature, but the sages of the Eastern calendar attribute to him characteristics such as thrift, enterprise, and the ability to undertake unexpected, unpredictable, non-conformist decisions." [8]

Klimov's metaphorical speech carried with it a caution. He recalled the collapse of Chukhrai's ETO, which was done in co-operation with the Donahue of Moscow television, Vladimir Posner.

"The slightest deviation from leaden stereotypes brought forth displeasure and accusation. It reminds me of a bad joke from the auto industry which as an experiment proposed right-hand drive," [9] said Klimov.

Beyond the Year of the Rabbit

Cinema, like literature, both reflects and reflects upon society. The art of politics is both a mirror of the people being governed and a molder of their dreams. Glasnost is as much a product of the Soviet people as it is of their leadership. What the policies portend for the future of humankind on this planet is a question of too large a scope for this book. Yet it is one that I would expect the reader will not be entirely able to avoid. George Orwell's *1984* tapped the fears of a world in the midst of technological change. His vision of the future did not come to pass and none of us would hope that Lopushansky's, in *Letters from a Dead Man,* will be prophetic.

Futuristic fantasies, recollections of past horrors, and the rude awakenings that come from graphic documentaries and docudrama may help to frame the consciousness of a better world. The first step is understanding.

The pendulum of artistic freedom in any state, East or West, is forever in motion. For the moment a cultural renaissance has occurred in the U.S.S.R., but it is too soon to tell if it will last. Its immediate effect is to bring Soviet cinema and society out of its xenophobic isolationism into the multi-national artistic environment and into the human community.

For the Soviet artist glasnost permits not only candor about the present and an honest reclamation of history, but also the rejuvenation of philosophical and religious perspectives drawn from the broad base of human experience.

"The appearance of Abuladze's *Repentance*," said critic Andrei Plakhov in *Soviet Film*, "provides evidence of the moral purification now taking place in Soviet society. Art is a potent means in this process." [10]

One should not construe from this that the Soviet Union is anything other than an officially atheist state, but the customs of the past do not die quickly. The U.S.S.R. is less than a century old. Russia was first Christianized ten centuries ago. Each Easter the churches are packed. On this day, believers and non-believers (even party members) exchange the ritual greeting, "Christ is Risen!"

The traditions of spirituality are woven deeply in the Russian psyche and language. This is the nation whose word for world, *mir*, is the same as that for peace.

In Voznesensky's poem "Fire in the Architectural Institute," the records of his misdemeanors are being consumed in flames. Today a chastening fire is burning in the film institutes as it once did for the poets of the Thaw.

"Is it the End?" asks Voznesensky.

"It's only the beginning."

"Let's go to the movies!" [11]

2 • *Youth In Turmoil*

*T*he scene is the Tilsi Home for Children, in the northern Soviet Republic of Estonia, where the hyperactive, emotionally brutalized offspring of alcoholics, incarcerated criminals and sexual abusers reside as wards of the state.

Mari Lehiste, a delicate girl of 16, who has been gang-raped in a railway station by Robi Samar and three other youths, is being interrogated. In this twisted world of psychological cripples, there is little room for truth or honest feelings. Deceit and mistrust are the order of the day, for truth would imply confrontation with grim reality and there are worse places than the children's homes. There are, for instance, the delinquent colonies. Mari, the victim, finds herself enthusiastically defending her assailant.

> *Investigator:* We are trying to keep Robi from criminal trouble. Will you help us?
> *Mari:* I'll try.
> *Investigator:* Two months ago, he was given a five-day pass to go home and you, in the meantime, met with him. Isn't that so? Where did you see him?
> *Mari:* At the railway station.
> *Investigator:* When?
> *Mari:* At night ... I mean, the evening.
> *Investigator:* When?
> *Mari:* Late at night.
> *Investigator:* So tell us what he wanted.
> *Mari:* Several drunken boys attacked me, but Robi protected me from them.

> **Investigator:** Ah! So that's the way it was. You're free to go now.
> **Mari:** Yes, but let me explain. There were four of them, four drunks, and Robi came in fighting like a tiger to save me.
> **Teacher:** I always knew Robi was better than he likes us all to believe.
> **Mari:** Everybody knows that. You think he's bad, but that's not true.

Mari's subterfuge doesn't work. Robi is committed to a delinquent colony. The police arrive and amid general pandemonium, the younger children of the home weep hysterically calling Robi's name. The older residents stand by stoically. The cacophonous sounds of wild creatures, cackling birds and droning insects are heard, and the melancholic atonal lament of a solo saxophone wails out as the doors to the paddy wagon close and Robi is spirited away.

Mari's interrogation and Robi's arrest are the climax of Leida Laius' *Games for Teenagers (Well, Come On, Smile)*, a feature length, color docudrama produced at the Tallinfilm Studio in Estonia. Tallinfilm is one of the newest Soviet studios. It produces only two or three features each year, but dozens of documentaries issue from its recently expanded film laboratories. *Games for Teenagers* is a stark exposé of the conditions in Soviet children's homes. It is also, like many other recent releases, a film about generational conflict. Mari can no more be honest with the older people of Tilsi than a prisoner can rat to the jailors. The positive role models provided by many of the adults at the orphanage in Nikolai Gubenko's 1977 Kiev Studio production, *The Orphans*, are not the stuff of the movies in the era of glasnost. The monolithic collective consciousness of Soviet society and the cinema that it reflects has changed. The people are examined as they really are—a cultural mosaic of individuals.

Films about youth each have their own method of mirroring the new national reality, but directors and scriptwriters share common aims in their willingness to explore what was previously verboten. Social maladjustment, lifestyles and attitudes outside the culturally accepted mainstream, even the dangers inherent in the state's own ideology, are examined. Laius' approach in *Games for Teenagers* is aggressive realism and docudrama. Vadim Abdrashitov in Mosfilm's *Plumbum, or A Dangerous Game* opts for black satire. Ruslan Chutko, the central character in the piece (nicknamed Plumbum) is a hard-eyed young ideologue, a kind of cinematic reincarnation of Pavlik Morozov, the child hero of the collectivization period. Morozov's commitment to ideology was so great that he turned in his own father, a kulak, to the

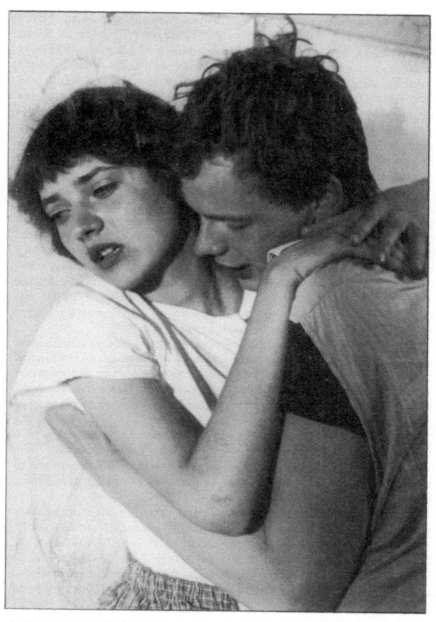

GAMES FOR TEENAGERS is a sympathethic but uncompromising view of victimized young people who live in an Estonian childrens' home. The film focuses on Mari, played by Monica Jarv (left), and her initiation into the home after her alcoholic father abandons her. (Photo: Courtesy Sovexportfilm)

Cheka for counter-revolutionary activities. After he was murdered by kulaks at the age of fourteen, Pavlik Morozov was held up to Soviet boys and girls as a role model. He became one of Stalin's pantheon of martyrs to socialism. Unlike Morozov, however, Ruslan does not enjoy the social status of a hero. In the Soviet Union of the '80s, a young man of Ruslan's character shares the same kind of social esteem as the Lyubers—the toughs from the Moscow suburb of Lyubertsy, who periodically descend on the city's *metalisty* (long-hairs, punks and rock music followers) much as the Mods and the Rockers collided at Britain's Brighton Beach in the '60s; that is, he is tolerated as ideologically sound by the authorities, but he is not liked by them.

The Lyubers, sons and daughters of blue-collar workers, may not be so talented or intellectual as Abdrashitov's young Chutko, but they have the same disdain for the world of adults and the same belief in their own purity. Their ideological perspective is at odds with the thrust of Gorbachev's *democratizatsia*, which holds respect for free expression not only in what people say, but also in how they appear. Toleration, however, may be difficult for Soviet society to accept. As Alexander Ivanov writing in the *Moscow News Weekly* observed in their 1987, 23rd edition: "With no habit, no tradition ... it's hard to learn democracy. Fierce clashes still lie in waiting for us on this road." [1]

When on May 4, 1987, police rounded up some fifty youths because older citizens in a Moscow neighborhood objected to their "hippie" demeanor, it was the police who were reprimanded for violating the young people's rights. The incident happened on Gogol Avenue, near Gorky Park, where long-haired youths gather each evening to play guitar, sing and converse.

"The militia patrol managed to violate the law, detaining youths who had committed no crimes," *Komsomolskaya Pravda* reported.[2] The Communist youth organ *Komsomolskaya Pravda*, which was once an arch-conservative voice, reads today, in the spirit of *novaya publicistika*, like a Soviet version of *Rolling Stone*.

The Lyubers and the *metalisty* are the extremes of contemporary young people. There is also the gray middle ground of aimless youth, without motivation, goals, or strong social values. Ivan Miroshnikov, the hero of Karen Shakhnazarov's lyrical comedy *The Messenger Boy*, is such a youth. Miroshnikov is the teenaged son of divorced parents who leaves school and takes a job as a courier, conscious that he will soon face, as all young U.S.S.R. males must, induction into the armed forces and possible service in Afghanistan. His laconic dry wit which mocks his elders had the audience rolling in the aisles when the movie previewed in Moscow.

Films such as Sergei Soloviev's Mosfilm production *ASSA* take us into the realm of the metalisty. *ASSA* is a tour-de-force montage of Soviet counter culture. Sergei Bugaev, who stars in the title role, plays with the Kino Rockers. Bugaev is the cult figure Captain Africa to whom the contemporary rock composer Boris Grebenshchikov, leader of Leningrad's Aquarium Rock Group, dedicated his popular song "I Call Captain Africa." The film features the best of Soviet rock groups, which were once forbidden to perform and operated underground. Elem Klimov made it clear in a Moscow news conference that Soloviev's work, as much as any other, *is* glasnost.

"It shows that there are no more taboos," he said. "We have no forbidden themes. That time is behind us—gone without a trace." [3]

The direction of the industry is illustrated as much by what is rejected as by the new themes that are promoted. The board of the Gorky Studio, Moscow's center for children's and youth cinema, recently turned down a proposal to make an animated version of Chekhov's story *Vanka Zhukov*. Their reasons can best be expressed as a series of questions. Why would young people be interested in the film? Of what relevance would it be to modern youth? And, even more to the point, what about the box office? Who will buy this film?

I spoke about the proposal with the respected young critic Irina Germanova.

"Youth today are activists—a generation of go-getters, public-minded and socially conscious in every sense," she said. "The Chekhov film wouldn't be interesting to them. They teach them about that in school. Forget it! Why doesn't this quiet, downtrodden individual protest against his oppressive environment, the children would think. Why doesn't he fight for happiness, rather than accept his fate passively?" [4]

I found Germanova frank and direct about her own life, about her society and about the gradual reclamation of cultural and literary heritage that has been occurring in the U.S.S.R. over the past two decades. Soviet readers may now, for instance, read Boris Pasternak and Vladimir Nabokov.

"It is now reasonable to expect that each successive generation will become and is becoming more and better educated, more informed and more knowledgeable in all fields," she said.

"In general, there is more information now about our contemporary world, about the West and about philosophers. All the things that my mother's generation was entirely deprived of, and that I myself was partially deprived of, are now coming to the surface."

"The process began in the educational system in the '60s. Dostoevsky was never taught in any school curriculum to my mother's generation, although I was introduced to his work."

"Now, however, youth finds itself in an entirely different cultural environment. There is a lot of translated literature appearing."

"The new generation understands things to which their parents had not even minimal informational access. Therefore their cognitive process is completely different."[5]

The New Raskolnikov: Dostoevsky Revisited

If Soviet production houses are hesitant to do remakes of the classic tales such as *Vanka Zhukov*, they are not afraid to draw upon classical themes. Together with the restoration of history and the boldly anti-Stalinist perspective of such works as *Repentance* there has come a reconsideration of the existential dilemma, a sifting of the literary themes of the past for clues to moral questions that do not rest neatly in the socialist-realist tradition.

Few films in a decade have generated as much controversy in the Soviet press and among cinema watchers in the U.S.S.R. as Abdrashitov's *Plumbum, or A Dangerous Game*. If Plumbum (Ruslan Chutko) is the cinematic incarnation of Pavlik Morozov, he is also an even darker monster. He is the new Raskolnikov (Dostoevsky's hero in *Crime and Punishment*). *Plumbum, or A Dangerous Game* has it all: generational conflict, anti-Stalinism, dark satire, and an existential theme that shatters the confinements of socialist realism.

Abdrashitov and his scriptwriter Alexander Mindadze, the creators of seven feature films, are noted for their terse style and cerebral themes. Their 1980 film *The Fox Hunt* broke ground as the first to show a non-heroic worker corrupted by his own society. They and other former students of film educator Mikhail Romm were also among the first to respond to the increased freedom offered directors and scriptwriters.

Plumbum (Ruslan Chutko) is an unsmiling, diminutive teenager with oversized ears and the seriousness of a 40-year-old. He lives in a small town with his liberal-minded, intellectual parents and goes to school where he is an honor student who receives a classical education and is considered a model citizen. His parents take pride in their son's achievements, unaware that he leads a secret life which is in conflict with their own.

The Chutkos are the intelligentsia of the 1960s, of the post-Stalinist Thaw period. They are romantic idealists whose views have not changed since the halcyon days of poetry when Yevgeni Yevtushenko and Andrei Voznesensky brought their message of euphoric hope and change to mass Soviet audiences. Their outlook, however, is not shared by the young Ruslan, who sees them as traitors in their society, naive dreamers who watch only blissful images on television, hold hands together and go skating. They fail to see the hopeless reality of corruption, unemployment, vagrancy and crime around them.

We find Ruslan with his admirer Sonia at the rink, where skaters glide by to a pop version of Beethoven's *Für Elise*. He is looking glum.

> *Sonia:* Did someone beat you up?
> *Ruslan:* Yes.
> *Sonia:* Who?
> *Ruslan:* This music...this goddamn music.
> *Sonia:* (starts to hum the tune) This is the most popular music around these days. You hear it everywhere.
> *Ruslan:* Shut up! Shut up! Don't you understand? Hear no evil. Speak no evil.
> *Sonia:* What's there to keep quiet about?
> *Ruslan:* In case it might be necessary to inform on someone, Mata Hari.
> *Sonia:* You have a double life. I've suspected it.

Ruslan does indeed lead a double life. Behind the facade of an exemplary youth, there lurks an idealogue cast from the same mold as Raskolnikov. Motivated by a perverse sense of justice, Ruslan seeks to rid society of what he sees as parasites: crooks, speculators, and black marketeers. He insinuates himself into the service of the criminal operational detachment of the city's police department. He penetrates the dens and hiding places of the underworld (called in Russian *malina*). He inspires the criminals to commit brilliantly conceived offenses and then he turns them over to the police. The innocent as well as the guilty become the victims of his zealous quest. In a direct parallel of Pavel Morozov, he incriminates his own father, who is caught fishing out of season. He destroys the career of Maria, the Magdelene-like figure and fashion model with whom he is infatuated, and at the climax of the film causes the death of Sonia, who has been drawn into his dangerous game.

In *Crime and Punishment*, Raskolnikov eliminates someone he perceives to be an undesirable in his murder of the old moneylender. But in pursuit of his ideal, he is forced also to kill the innocent, accidental witness to the crime the half-wit Lizaveta. Abdrashitov in *Plumbum, or A Dangerous Game* mirrors the Dostoevskian theme in his final scene, when Ruslan, the teenaged superman, determines to eliminate a hooligan who has stolen his tape recorder. In the rooftop struggle that ensues, Sonia plummets to her death.

PLUMBUM, OR A DANGEROUS GAME: The hero of Vadim Abdrashitov's *Plumbum* is an unsmiling, diminutive teenager with oversized ears and the seriousness of a 40–year–old. (Poster: Courtesy Sovexportfilm)

Raskolnikov, like Ruslan, is a keenly superior student. He concocts an essay which divides humankind into two forms—the heroes and the vast mass. Out of the mass, the hero might emerge perhaps one in a thousand times. He believes himself to be such a man. He is, he thinks, by intellectual birthright above society and above the law, capable of acting as Napoleon might have done. He sees a landscape of black and white, of good and evil, and himself like Nietzsche's Ubermensch beyond all mores. Ruslan's world similarly has no shades of meaning. In a symbolic scene, the young Chutko imagines his perfect universe as he observes a dance class of beautiful women in white dresses and men in formal black waltzing to the music of Strauss. His utopia has no nuances, no complex relationships, no mercy, no forgiveness and no compassion. If Raskolnikov's great man is Napoleon, then Ruslan's progenitor is Stalin.

Abdrashitov's film is a bold departure from Soviet cinema's socialist realist roots. In the past, Ruslan, the man of action, the self-styled reformer who seeks to change society and is not afraid to use force to further his end, would have been a positive hero. Socialist realism portrayed the virtues of ideology. In *Plumbum, or A Dangerous Game,* its hazards are exposed in the broader existential perspective.

Abdrashitov's intention is manifested in a debate between Grayhead, the chief of detectives, and the young fanatic. Ruslan's nickname (Plumbum) means, not coincidentally, lead. Stalin was known as the Man of Steel. The police have just completed a raid which Ruslan helped to engineer, but the chief of detectives, who has more life experience than the teenager, is suspicious of his purpose. It is reminiscent of Raskolnikov's battle of wits with the police inspector Porfiry. Raskolnikov thinks he can commit the perfect crime. Ruslan thinks he has the perfect solution.

> **Ruslan:** Don't you have any questions?
> **Grayhead:** Only one. Why are you called Lead?
> **Ruslan:** Well, why are you called Grayhead?
> **Grayhead:** Isn't Plumbum the same as lead ... a soft metal? (He laughs patronizingly.) I would understand, if it were steel.
> **Ruslan:** Steel? That has other connotations.

Plumbum, or A Dangerous Game, said critic Irina Germanova during our interview, exemplifies the failure of both parents and the educational system to keep up with the complexities of social change.

"Classical concepts inculcated in the adolescent mind at school cannot be appreciated until one has lived through all the circumstances,"[6] she said.

Ruslan, who is three generations from the Stalinist era, cannot hope to understand its reality.

"Plumbum is the frightening product of a harsh world view. The film is in concept a very serious one. The reason is that there is a vast number of such youths in our society. Plumbum is soft, though of metallic fibre. He can be easily molded and he is heavy in the sense that his conscience brings the burden of revenge on all who do not fit his image of the ideal." [7]

What Do You Want to Do with Your Life, Ivan Miroshnikov?

Cast aside now the heady contemplation of supermen, of dark messages and anti-Stalinist innuendo. Look at the dilemmas of contemporary youth through the eyes of Ivan Miroshnikov, the comic protagonist of Karen Shakhnazarov's *The Messenger Boy.* Think about failing your entrance exam to teacher's college and consider that most difficult of quandaries for the young, urban male: where, oh where, in the Union of Soviet Socialist Republics can you find a place, any place, to get-it-on with your girlfriend? The problem is formidable. The backseat of the family car won't do. Unless your family is part of the elite (and Ivan's isn't), you don't have a family car. They won't leave you alone in the rec room on a Saturday night—you don't have one of those either. If you are Ivan, you live in an apartment with your divorced mother. You have a small room, but mother sleeps on the sofa-bed in the living room. The solution in a moment. First cogitate on this one; it's the question everyone seems to ask these days: "Ivan, what do you want to do with your life?"

The Messenger Boy traces the passage of the young Miroshnikov from his skate-boarding, break-dancing adolescence through his adjustment to the working world and his first zany encounter with the opposite sex. The boy's ironic view of the older generation permeates the film. Ivan is a leg-puller whose taunts and one-liners do more than just poke fun.

They test the values of the adult world he encounters, ridicule the social strata of his supposedly classless society and even scoff at the national ideology. All this he delivers with an expressionless voice and a deadpan face that make him irresistible. Here are some examples of his disrespect.

Begin with a job résumé.

Résumé

I was born in the province of Longado in 1668. The family belonged
to one of the most noble in the kingdom, the Ebresacs, who fought
in the service of Holland and of whose members one was wounded.
There I lived with my mother, the Baroness du Monjou, until the age
of 17. I received a good upbringing and a fairly decent education.
After leaving my parents, I was listed as a member of the Elite Black-
guards in the service of His Imperial Majesty.

Despite his whimsy, Ivan gets the job. He becomes a courier for the
scientific journal *Voprosy Poznaniya* and his first task is to deliver a
manuscript to the plush flat of a celebrated scientist, Professor Semyon
Petrovich Kuznetsov. For Ivan it's a chance to make a pass at the
professor's svelte daughter, Katya. The professor, played by veteran
actor Oleg Basilashivili, lectures Ivan on the benefits of study and hard
work.

> **Kuznetsov:** It's a question of principles. I . . . We . . . Our generation
> wants to know for whom we have lived and fought, into whose
> hands will fall the legacy of all our knowledge? I am curious about
> the principles by which you propose to exist in society.
> **Ivan:** My principles are simple ones. I'd like to have ... a car, an
> apartment in the center of town, a *dacha** in the country and yes ...
> to work as little as possible.
> **Kuznetsov:** First you must earn these things. No one will give you a
> car or a dacha, just like that. You will have to work hard, acquire
> some skills and some knowledge. There is no other way.
> **Ivan:** Why not? What if I were to get married? Say to your
> daughter; she would become my wife and there you have it in the
> bag. Connections. Plenty of money. Do you really have it in your
> heart to make your only daughter miserable? You could find me a
> job at the institute, some nice, warm place, and perhaps buy us an
> apartment.

The scene is reminiscent of the poolside conversation between Dustin
Hoffman and a middle-aged businessman in *The Graduate*: "Plastics,"
the man tells him.

Ivan eventually charms Katya, but first consider the example he gets
from the adults at the editorial office. There's Zina, for instance, the

---

* dacha, a summer cottage

THE MESSENGER BOY: This lyrical comedy, deftly directed by Karen Shakhnazarov, presents the passage to manhood of Ivan Miroshnikov, a former schoolboy, who takes his first job as a courier for *Voprosy Poznaniya*. The youth's dry laconic wit which mocks his elders had audiences rolling in the aisles when the film previewed in Moscow. (Photo: Courtesy Sovexportfilm)

bleached blonde secretary, who is single and wiles away the working day dreaming of the perfect man (preferably Japanese, because they are the most technologically advanced). Stepan Afanasievich Makarov, the assistant editor, would rather be fishing.

> *Zina:* Stepan Afanasievich, what is your greatest wish in life?
> *Stepan:* I wish that the barometric pressure wouldn't keep dropping . . . the fish would bite better.
> *Zina:* (upset) I'm being serious. How about you, Ivan?
> *Ivan:* My dream is that world communism will triumph.

Ivan's disrespectful punchline provoked similar irreverence in Moscow audiences. No line in the film produced such uproarious laughter as this one.[8] Parlor-room and working-place humor which mocks the political establishment has long been a part of everyday Soviet life. With *The Messenger Boy* it is shown at last on the screen. So how does our hero get his girl? It isn't easy. In Ivan's ultimate put-on triumph, the young courier convinces the gullibly earnest Professor Kuznetsov that Katya is expecting a child.

"Would it be all right if I call you dad from now on?" he asks.

The rebellious Katya plays along with the ruse. The only solution she suggests is to "get a baby," but how, or more to the point, where? Ivan's idea, the entranceway to Moscow University, won't do. The park won't do. They are interrupted there by an older couple.

"Are you a man or a dog-dropping? Do something!" Katya screams. "Find an apartment. Phone a friend."

Ivan has a friend, but what he provides is the key to a musty cellar where the pipes are leaking. As the consummate moment arrives, so does the plumber.

"Degenerates," he shouts. "And in broad daylight too!"

The Messenger Boy is as much a portrait of three generations as it is a story of Ivan. Attitudes formed in the Great Patriotic War, in the Thaw and in the Age of Perestroika are tightly interwoven in Alexander Borodyansky's script.

To Katya's grandmother, today's youth are "wonderful, heroic even."

Ivan's mother, played by Inna Churikova (the U.S.S.R.'s most popular screen actress), is a daughter of the Thaw. The turning point in her life, she tells her son, was when she read some Voznesensky poems at an acting audition in the '60s. Her forté was comedy. Reading Voznesensky was a poor choice: it finished her career.

The youth in the film are indicative of the pluralism of the '80s. Bazin, Ivan's closest friend, is an idler whose idea of adapting to life is hanging out on street corners and tuning in via his ghetto blaster. Katya and her friends are the privileged few who can look forward to the benefits of international travel, luxuries and fine clothes. The hero finds the values of all of them bewildering. He and others must find their path through self-discovery. Katya breaks off with Ivan, returning to her fantasies of owning a sports car and an exotic dog. Bazin's wish is more pedestrian. He wants a new winter coat. In the concluding scene, he gets it. The protagonist removes his own coat and gives it to his friend.

"Now you can dream of greater things," says Ivan. Miroshnikov's future stands before him in the person of a young soldier, fresh from Afghanistan, wearing the face of war and the white sash signifying his service to his country. Ivan no longer requires his coat. The army will provide one.

Miroshnikov's quest, like that of the cosmonaut Ivan Naidenov in Soloviev's *Wild Pigeon* discussed in Chapter 3, originates in his own internal universe. What distinguishes *The Messenger Boy,* as much as its use of humor as a means of social commentary, is this individualized approach. The film is indicative of just how drastically comedy, and indeed all of Soviet cinema, has changed in response to glasnost.

One way of looking at what has come into being from the wellspring of a new social consciousness is to take a brief journey through the keyhole of cinematic history.

Looking Back:
The Orphans (1977),
Ivan Brovkin (1955, 1959)

If there is hope for the characters in *The Messenger Boy* and in Leida Laius' *Games for Teenagers (Well, Come on, Smile),* it lies in their ability to think for themselves rather than relying on collective answers. *The Orphans (Wounded Game),* produced only a decade before, like Leida Laius' film, portrays children exiled from normal family lives. But in Gubenko's film, the adults rescue the children and through their communal efforts create a future for them. The good-for-nothing Gomer Pyle-like, comic hero of Ivan Lukinsky's 1955 Gorky Studio production *The Soldier, Ivan Brovkin* and its sequel *Ivan Brovkin on the State Farm (1959)* needs the help of the entire Soviet army to make a man of him. He suffers from the same excesses as Miroshnikov—defiance of authority, an overactive libido, and a charismatic (if somewhat folksy) wit. But the humor is situational as Brovkin single-handedly brings a *kolkhoz** to its knees, before he is

---

* kolkhoz, collective farm.

drafted into the army and is redeemed by the teamwork of battle maneuvers.

Attitudes changed in American cinema when directors began to acknowledge with *Easy Rider, Rebel Without a Cause,* and *Midnight Cowboy* that heroes are not necessarily positive social role models and that the good guys don't always win. Glasnost for the Soviet cinema means something similar—the right to show despair in words, in images and in sound.

The Orphans and *Games for Teenagers* both make significant use of bird noises to develop their themes. In Gubenko's work, set in an orphanage in post-war Odessa, the birds contribute a sense of hope and even humor, while in Laius' production the jungle-like, mocking sounds of birds and insects put the viewer on edge and heighten the mood of isolation and despair. *The Orphans* is a traditional Soviet treatment, built around a primary symbol—the birds. Their significance can be found in the Russian title, *Podranki,* which literally means *Wounded Game.* The characters in the film have been wounded by war. The message we receive is that, like wounded birds, the Russian people were forced to learn to fly again. The people cannot remain trapped within the memory of war, they must go on, to wallow is to court disaster, and the best road to renewal is through helping one another. The setting here is not the sterile, modern, institutional setting of the Tilsi Home. The orphanage in Gubenko's film is a rambling rural estate where the residents discover and artists renovate antiquarian frescoes.

Alyosha, the central character of *The Orphans,* is shown sifting garbage for scraps of food. He and other war waifs are no more than animals abandoned amid smoking rubble and lean-to shacks. His teachers are disabled veterans, kindly women and old men who are victims of the war themselves. They are the vehicle through which all the things that people are supposed to love are re-established. Alyosha, the fallen bird, finds his wings again, matures and grows into manhood with an appreciation of art, literature and music. Leida Laius has no need for such symbolism; reality is for her enough and hope has no place in her scenario.

Karen Shakhnazarov, in *The Messenger Boy,* addresses the same theme but with a lighter, more humorous, touch. *The Messenger Boy* and the Brovkin films are popular lyrical comedies. They capture the spirit of their time through the experience of a unique teenager. Brovkin, like Miroshnikov, is involved with a girl beyond his social reach, the kolkhoz chairman's daughter, but in Brovkin's cinematic world dreams come true. He wins the girl. They marry. Lukinsky's hero is a sentimental klutz who perpetually becomes the victim of cruel fate—pig pen cleaning, confinement to barracks and hundreds of push-ups. He, not his environment, is the brunt of the joke. For Brovkin the question is not, what do you want to do with your life, but what can society possibly do with you?

Miroshnikov, by contrast, has no one to rely on but himself. His inner spirit, and that alone, is the source of his redemption. His father is in Africa. His mother is absorbed in her own loneliness. He finds no fulfillment among his peers.

Miroshnikov's identity is discovered in surreal fantasies of Masai warriors in their rites of passage. In the landscape of desolation, invoked by the primitive strains of an African flute, they track a leopard over barren dunes: outcasts, who cannot return to their tribe until their hunt is complete.

In his inner journey, Miroshnikov confronts the social order and by drawing his own conclusions, he transcends it. Plumbum also draws his own conclusions, but he would force society to stand on its head. Alyosha is nurtured by his teachers. Mari is the victim of her educational setting. Plumbum, Miroshnikov, and Mari—three individuals from the cultural mosaic of the '80s—each one of them is at loggerheads with the older generation. They tread a path not created by the goodwill and support of their society, but by the disorder and disintegration they find around them. They are from different social strata, but each is socially aware and activist in his or her own way: Plumbum by taking the law into his own hands, Miroshnikov by using his wit which challenges his elders, Mari by defending her generation even at the cost of her own dignity.

Directors with Commitment

Soviet directors, like the young people they portray, are often activists themselves. They carry their involvement with youth beyond the movie set and the cutting room floor into other parts of their lives. Sergei Soloviev, the director of *ASSA*, teaches film at VGIK, tutors the creative group Debut at the Mosfilm studio and, as one of the secretaries of SFU, heads up the young directors' section. Leida Laius, of *Games for Teenagers (Well, Come On, Smile)*, has become involved with state officials and educators in the Estonian Republic, and with conferences in Southern Russia and in Central Asia in an attempt to change conditions in Soviet children's homes.

I met Soloviev with Pyotr Lucyk, the VGIK Komsomol representative, over *okroshka** and pickled herring in the restaurant at Dom

---

* *Okroshka*, cold fermented soup.

Kino, SFU's headquarters, which houses the SFU and PROK (Professional Club), where the who's who of Soviet cinema congregate. Lucyk, a scriptwriter, was involved on a day-to-day basis with the changes brought by perestroika.

"It was almost impossible at one time for young filmmakers to have a career," Lucyk said. "There was a contingent of directors who had achieved a certain status and blocked the way of many talented voices. The re-organized studios, on the contrary, are interested in the new cadres. There has been a dramatic change from the point of view of accessibility, of new ideas, new blood and commercialism." [9]

Soloviev, who is in his forties, wrote the script for *ASSA* in collaboration with 22-year-old dramatist Sergei Livnev. According to Soloviev: "Livnev was not only a partner, but also a consultant on the culture of 20-year-olds, which is light years away from me and my generation."

The rock music for the film, composed by Boris Grebenshchikov, is in Soloviev's view distinctly Soviet.

"It has grown out of Soviet realities. It may be harsh and grating, but only because it shatters outdated, meaningless stereotypes."

"Its absurdism continues indirectly the traditions of Russian and Soviet literature. It is profoundly original, national and socially committed," [10] he said.

Leida Laius is a self-assertive, purposeful woman in her sixties, who has the vitality of someone 20 years younger and exudes an empathy that cuts across the generations. She clearly approached the filming of *Games for Teenagers* with a sense of mission. Many of the original scenes were created by recording real-life situations with hidden cameras and microphones and with the director performing in the guise of a street person, or sometimes a social worker. This was the starting point for Maria Sheptunova's simple but compelling script. Laius, Sheptunova, and cinematographer/co-director Arvo Iho formed a collective to travel across Estonia gathering material.

"What we discovered was so shocking that we felt it had to be treated with the utmost seriousness," Laius told me. "From start to finish, the theme screamed at us. We knew that we must reveal what is not commonly known—what lies behind the scenes." [11]

She had originally hoped to have children from the homes perform their own life stories, or at least those of their peers. This proved impractical. They were too shackled by their own circumstances to face the trauma of leading roles.

A compromise was struck. The main characters were played by children selected from grades 9 and 10 at various schools in the city of Tallin, Estonia's capital. But all the supporting parts were acted by residents of the Tilsi Home. Many months after the shooting, Laius was still writing personal letters to some of the young people at the home and at her insistence the movie received its first showing there.

"We had to view the film on the most substandard of screens, but the whole thing was received with the most joyous delight," she said. "The children recognized themselves, but most of all, they recognized the director of the home." The actor who played this part modelled himself after the administrator of Tilsi. He copied his prototype so carefully that he even mimicked the man's limp. "When the children saw this, they burst into spontaneous laughter." [12]

"When I talked to them afterwards, their mood had changed. That was when all their pent up emotions came out. I tried to impress on them that they would have to rely entirely on their own resources, their own strength, when they were leaving the home. This is the conclusion that I have come to about these places, that the children can only help themselves by relying on their own efforts." [13]

The prognosis, however, is not good. Neither Laius' film nor the results of her subsequent research paint a bright picture.

"Most of the children from homes such as Tilsi will receive only a grade 8 education. A minute proportion of the most gifted will go on to high school. The rest may go on to trade schools. Most will wind up as farm workers, tractor drivers, seamstresses, or in more mundane jobs. Over half of them will be unable to cope and will wind up in trouble with the law. They let them out of the homes with 10 rubles and the prospect of further training (a month's rent is 18 rubles), but feeling their freedom for the first time, they have difficulty standing on their own feet. In the home at least they were provided with food and shelter."

Mari, the heroine of Games for Teenagers, is committed to Tilsi after her self-centered, divorced, father rejects her. Initially she remains aloof and doesn't want to get involved with the others whom she sees as different from herself. But by the end of the film, she has received a very special education, the kind that only such places as Tilsi can provide. She has learned to adapt, she has been socialized by the institution and by the other victims who share her fate. She is part of a new family and the bond that links her to it is mutual misery. In a touching scene, a sad ten-year-old, Kerttu, who has been at Tilsi for some time, plans to escape. To accomplish this feat, she believes she must find a way to acquire a passport. The document is the only thing she thinks is necessary to live in society. Her belief is based on the one childish recollection she has of life outside the home.

For all the Kerttus and Maris in Soviet children's homes, chances are, if she could, Leida Laius would invent such a passport.

3 • *Odysseys In Inner Space*

You are a long way from home. You circle the globe in a satellite and you float weightless—free. The blue sphere of Earth is below you. Then you see it, a tiny speck on the face of the mother planet, the town where you were raised.

To look at the world from this perspective is objectively to see it as Ivan Naidenov, the cosmonaut-hero of Soloviev's biographical feature *Wild Pigeon* sees it. But what Ivan Naidenov sees is more than a speck on the face of Planet Earth. As he circles Earth, listening to the clock tick in the capsule, he takes an odyssey in inner space, a trip into the shadowy realm of childhood recollection.

The year is 1946. The location is Aktyubinsk, a small settlement in Kazakhstan. The Great Patriotic War has just ended and a bizarre obsession grips the nation—a craze for pigeons. Amid the wreckage of deserted factories and abandoned aircraft, Ivan is on a quest as strange as the mythological one for the Holy Grail. It is a quest for the White One.

The White One is a rare winged beauty. A pigeon mafia, whose membership includes a corrupt cop, a black marketeer, a character known only as the Gypsy and another whose pseudonym is the Colonel, are willing to kill or be killed to possess her.

Sergei Soloviev's Kazakhfilm/Mosfilm production *Wild Pigeon* is a multi-layered motion picture. It is at once symbolical yet rooted in concrete historical reality. The pigeon craze was real. It swept across a war-ravaged Soviet Union much as the hula hoop phenomenon captured the imagination of American consumer society in the affluent '50s. Soloviev's answer to me in response to questions about the film illustrates the contrast between East and West.

"It was horrible. It was inexplicable," Soloviev told me. "The whole country was pigeon happy. The mania became so intense that the people caught up in it, many of whom were gangsters and hooligans, were prepared to kill over it." [1]

Naidenov too is real and these are his actual boyhood recollections, yet the film is more than a simple biographical study. This work and others of its genre, Alexei Gherman's *My Friend Ivan Lapshin* and Gleb Panfilov's *Theme* are representative of a new perspective in Soviet film—cinematic introspection.

The approach first began to transform the medium in the '70s. It was, like all perspectives that challenge the confines of conventional thought, initially suspect. *Theme* was banned for seven years. *My Friend Ivan Lapshin* suffered from a limited release of only a handful of prints, then was shelved for two years. *Wild Pigeon* is a product of the Gorbachev era and hence did not suffer the same repression.

The focus of the new art is the human psyche, human perception in the midst of socio-political change—the subjective experience in history. It is a subtle form, rich in structural contrast and literary allusion, founded in the technique of artistic distancing.

Soloviev's hero, Ivan Naidenov, exists in two time frames. He is both adult narrator (Naidenov) and child protagonist (Gray). Adrift in space, he is as far from his fellow human beings as any living soul may be and from his distant looking post he tunes in on a world of brutish reminiscence. Grown men and children alike are prepared to risk all for a white pigeon, while in the sub-plot Ivan's father (Pavel), a shell-shocked and brain-damaged war veteran, becomes the brunt of cruel practical jokes; and the woman he loves, a former Moscow actress (Xenia), commits suicide after she is accused of speculation for selling her coat to survive.

Kim Yesenin, the hero of Gleb Panfilov's psychological drama *Theme*, like Ivan Naidenov, takes both an inner and an outer odyssey. The film is a graphic representation of the life of the writer during the post-Thaw era, now described as "the period of stagnation," and was filmed in that era (1979). Yesenin, a hardened urban playwright, leaves behind the familiar turf of Moscow to travel to the Vladimir-Suzdal region where the spires and the cupolas of a Christian architecture dating from thirteenth century rise above the pastoral landscape. The region was, for the eight centuries prior to the revolution, a center of Russian cultural achievement. It was the birthplace of saints and of art forms that are now regarded as a national treasury. In the icons and the tapestries and the buildings conserved here we may find Russia's roots, her living past.

Here Yesenin hopes to find the theme for a new play, and perhaps an inner rebirth. What he has chosen to research is *The Song of Prince Igor's Campaign*, a record of Prince Igor Svyatoslavovich's disastrous

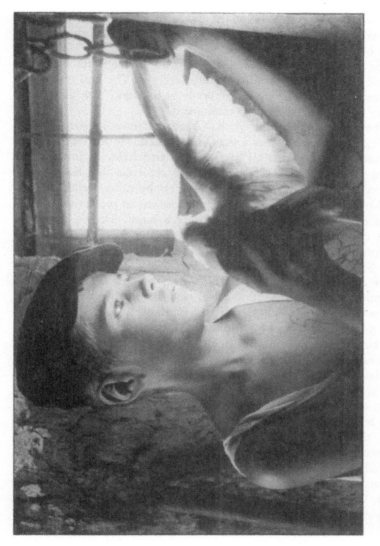

WILD PIGEON: In the post-war U.S.S.R., the nation was overwhelmed by a craze for pigeons. Here Ivan Naidenov, the boy-hero of Soloviev's film *Wild Pigeon*, is shown with the White One—the prize which every pigeon fancier seeks. (Photo: Courtesy Sovexportfilm).

military pursuits and his defeat at the hands of the nomadic Polovtsy. *The Song* is the motherland's first recorded literature. It is the Russian equivalent of *Beowulf.*

"It's the perfect story," Yesenin thinks to himself. Its classical, nationalistic subject matter will be readily accepted. The box office will be guaranteed and it will play in hundreds of theaters. "I'm an old cat but I haven't yet forgotten how to catch mice."

When he arrives in Vladimir-Suzdal, Yesenin's inner journey begins. His identity as a writer and as a man is assaulted. He realizes that his theme is hackneyed and that his life has been artistically fraudulent. He has the support of the state. He has received accolades, but he has sold his integrity. He is led to his artistic awareness by other writers he encounters—provincial scribes who have no prospects of recognition.

Almost everyone in this film is writing a book. There's Yesenin's travelling companion, the detective story writer Yevgeni Pashchin. There's Andrei, the Jewish gravedigger-poet, who, readers will recall from our brief discussion in Chapter 1, sees life as death "in a country where one cannot practice the art which gives one life." There's Sasha, the museum guide, who is writing a biography of the obscure, eccentric poet, Alexander Yegorovich Chizhikov (Chizhik). And then there's Yuri, the poet/traffic cop, who vies with Yesenin for Sasha's attention. Chizhik, by the way, is dead, but he's the only real writer in the script. The rest are fictional. Chizhik lived in Palekh, the small heartland town near Suzdal which is renowned for its miniature lacquer work. He was self-taught, an alcoholic who survived by working as a fireman, yet his prophetic verse written in the gnarled idiom of the hinterland had a primitive but evocative vitality. It is Chizhik's poetry and a confrontation with the intelligent and committed Sasha which leads Yesenin to artistic awareness and impresses upon him how truly far he is from his cultural roots.

"You are spiritually dead," Sasha tells him at a dinner party given in his honor. "You write plays for Komsomols.* What do you know about Prince Igor?"

Ironically, Sasha herself will not rise above her status as a museum guide. Her society will allow her to pick the bones of the creative dead, but will not allow her to create herself. For her and for the other writers portrayed in the film, there is no exit from creative stagnation and repression.

The traffic cop, Yuri, despite his sincere love of literature and his pas-

---

* Komsomols, Communist Youth. The hero's name *Kim* is an acronym for the youth movement *Kommunisticheskii Internatsional Molodezhi.*

sion for writing which he terms his "graphomania," can publish only amateurish poems and letters to the editor. Andrei, the Jew, is literally and symbolically a gravedigger. By his commitment to his own sense of truth, he digs his own grave. He assigns himself to oblivion and the only solution is to emigrate, but to do so is to abandon his country. Yesenin, in the final scenes, tries to escape, to find a way out, but his inner conflict gets the better of him.

On the highway returning to Moscow, Yesenin realizes that he cannot go back to his privileged but artistically compromised life in the capital. In a frenzy he turns his vehicle around. It rolls. It bursts into flames. Battered and burnt, the hero struggles to a phone booth to call Sasha. As she answers, he collapses.

Gherman's Time Machine

Dostoevsky, while he was travelling abroad, said to Turgenev that if he really wanted to see Russia, he should get himself a telescope. Turgenev had then settled in the West. In Dostoevsky's view, Turgenev had so distanced himself from Russian society that he could not possibly understand it.

Dostoevsky's jibe at his literary rival misses the mark. Turgenev, from the distance of France, was an acute observer and his distancing was the source of his perceptiveness. The writer does indeed look at Russia as if through a telescope and what he sees comes sharply into focus. He presents things as they are without judgement. By contrast, Dostoevsky and Tolstoy, the two other literary giants of the 19th century, preach to their readers. They seek to convert. They are not content to be observers.

The filmmakers Sergei Soloviev, Alexei Gherman and Gleb Panfilov share with Turgenev the clarity of vision that comes from distancing.

Soloviev in *Wild Pigeon* distances his narrator in time and space from the action of the film. In the vacuum of the orbiting space capsule, he is pure mind, pure subjectivity. Panfilov in *Theme* distances his protagonist from the comfort of Moscow and places him in a white-walled hinterland community, in winter, when everything (the fences, the buildings and the land) is white. The ancient pristine purity of the setting contrasts sharply with the contemporary emotional turmoil of the characters.

Each artist—Soloviev, Panfilov and Gherman—uses the flickering images of the celluloid medium to express a conception of time, of space and of human experience that is larger than dogma or ideology. It is a perspective which is at once relativistic, yet universal and more phenomenological than rationalistic. Gherman's approach is the most radical of the three, the most creatively profound and the most idiosyncratic.

Soloviev takes us to Naidenov's irrational inner world through the devices of a structured art—an art which has as its framework the quest for the White One. What Gherman does in *My Friend Ivan Lapshin* is to make art by its irrational ordering mirror reality.

Gherman sets aside conventional structure. In this film, which is an elaborate interweaving of fact and fiction, of reality and illusion, it is the director, his camera and the audience who take an odyssey. The scenes pass before us like those viewed through a train window. Characters emerge but one cannot be sure what they are doing or why they are there. Snatches of conversation, objects, occurrences, flash on screen disconnectedly. There is none of the satisfaction and edification that comes from structured art. The viewers are distanced, forced to suspend themselves in the pure experience of observation.

Alexei Gherman's film is based on his father Yuri Gherman's short stories. The setting is an isolated port city in 1935—the fictional Unchansk. The plot, if that is an appropriate word, is a detective story developed through voice-over narration. The film was shot in Astrakhan on the Volga Basin, but nothing in it would connect us with the locale. The location is left deliberately obscure.

"We lived on the outskirts of our country—a half a minute's walk from here and a half a century ago," says the narrator.

In 1935, the Stalinist purges were beginning, and our hero is an NKVD policeman, but the film shows little of the great events of the epoch. The point of view is distinctly apolitical—neutral. Stalin's portrait appears in the film, but with equal prominence we also see that of Stalin's victim Sergei Kirov.[*] Stalin's picture appears to the beat of a marching band, plastered on the front of a tram. When Kirov's image is shown, the soundtrack is marked by a drumbeat like the shot that dispatched him from this world. Executioner and prey are one in Gherman's universe. Both are but a part of the scenery.

We see too, in a scene which shocks, some of the other victims of this violent era—dead bodies, caked with ice, dragged ingloriously from a ditch. Yet though the viewer may be shocked, it is impossible to feel empathy for the dead. They are undeveloped characters. The viewer has

---

[*] Kirov, the powerful Leningrad Party Chief, who inspired Stalin's jealousy. His 1934 assassination was the prelude to the great purges of 1936-1938. It has long been contended that the murder was engineered by the NKVD, at Stalin's direction.

had no previous contact with them. In Unchansk, the living and the dead are but common souls lost in the panorama of time.

Ivan Lapshin and the other members of the NKVD Criminal Investigations Division are on the lookout for the mass-murderer Soloviev (no relation to the director Sergei Soloviev) who had been sentenced to death in Turkestan, has escaped and is reported to be in the area. Soloviev is an historical figure. Here we have the foundation for a first-class detective thriller. But this is not what we get. There are no high speed chases in this film. There is no intrigue and no dramatic tension. We see Soloviev only near the end of the film when Lapshin guns him down. The director focuses instead on the texture of the time—the history of ordinary experience.

The dress, the mannerisms and the social attitudes of the '30s in a provincial backwater town are reproduced with anthropological authenticity. We look at them as if through the viewfinder of a 70 mm time machine.

Before the lens the figures go about their affairs as if they were unaware that they were being observed. The camera in real time may move continuously from ceiling to floor following them, never missing a beat, but if the camera stops, the actors glide by unaware of the parameters of the photographic frame which would organize them. Sometimes the characters stop too and stare directly at the camera with all the innocence of the naïve candids captured in early documentaries and newsreels. The scene continues in the background. On the screen all is change, all is perpetual historical motion. As with Hegel's view of history, there is no pat resolution—the panorama moves on.

Gherman's time-machine approach, like Sergei Soloviev's space capsule device, creates a uchronia, a special no-time zone, an absolute periphery. He invents an hermetic, lifelike, fictional space which demystifies history and modulates time. Unchansk is a hypothetical black hole that seals within itself a universe which is witness to another dimension. The characters and their adventures in Unchansk are shown as if they had existed and still exist, and we can reach them through the magic of cinematography.

The obliviousness of the characters to the outcome of evolving time makes Gherman's overview all the more poignant. That which is becoming for them attains meaning only in the subjective dream. The characters are as naïve about the present as they are about the future.

"I don't believe that Mayakovsky killed himself. It's just another rumor," says Lapshin's journalist friend Khanin.

Vladimir Mayakovsky was of course the great revolutionary poet who dedicated his work to the service of party and country. In his last significant poem, *At the Top* of My Voice, composed in 1930, he wrote:

Agitprop*
> sticks
>> in my teeth too,
> and I'd rather
>> compose
>>> romances for you—
> more profit in it
>> and more charm.

But I
> subdued
>> myself,
>>> setting my heel
> on the throat
>> of my own song. [2]

As Lapshin is closing in on Soloviev, a bystander asks about the criminal's motivation for the crimes. No ideological motives are given. "What motivation?" says Lapshin. "He's just a murderer, that's all." Lapshin sees Soloviev as scum and his mission in life is to rid the world of such undesirables. International Workers Day is coming. He hopes to fulfill his quota of arrests in time. Lapshin is a worker like any other with a job to do. He lives for the better world that he hopes he may have some part in creating. The characters in Unchansk are caught up in a drama which they regard as having some end. They complain of the present, but the end justifies it. They possess a dream that they actually believe will come into being.

"We will clear the land of scum," Lapshin says repeatedly. "We will plant an orchard and we will still have time to stroll in it."

There is some larger retrospective social irony in the fact that over the next few years the NKVD would participate in the purging of millions of their fellow citizens for political reasons. But that is not Lapshin's concern.

His duty is to track down criminals and like any police officer anywhere in the world he does it the best he can. He believes in what he does and the measure of his success is the number of arrests he makes.

When Lapshin finally meets Soloviev, however, it could be a scene from a Charles Bronson flick. Soloviev surrenders, casting his weapon

---

* **AGITPROP.** The Agitation and Propaganda Section of the Party's Central Committee.

aside, putting his hands up, but Lapshin dispenses instant justice with a deadly blast from his rifle.

Gherman's detective and his generation lived for the future. The characters in the film avoid the old, wooden sidewalks—the way of the past. They prefer to take the long way home, through the park, under the newly constructed archway. They stand beneath banners on a garlanded dock to greet a new passenger vessel which has been assigned to their port. The whole town gathers. It would be a sign of shame not to be there. Brass bands play. The community shares a childlike optimism.

With films such as *My Friend Ivan Lapshin*, *Wild Pigeon* and *Theme*, Soviet filmmakers have arrived at an historical maturity. They no longer clean up the past to make it fit the mold of an outdated aesthetic.

The heroes of these films are not larger-than-life creations, models to mobilize the masses in the struggle for building communism, but ordinary people caught in their temporal circumstances. Their inner experiences have a national character, but the artistic viewpoint of the filmmakers is not one that can be easily contained by ethnocentric boundaries. It has more in common with the Western cinema of filmmakers such as Goddard, with the thrust of modern Western philosophy, from Husserl to Heidegger to Sartre, than it does with the idealized aesthetic of socialist realism.

At last it has been recognized that 1917 was a long time ago. Several generations have since grown up and some have passed away. Most of the revolutionaries from 1917 are dead. Soviet society is now made up largely of their grandchildren.

Citizens living in the '20s and '30s, except for the very old, tended not to think about the past. History, for them, had essentially come to an end with the storming of the Winter Palace. The Lenin and Stalin generations lived for the future—the orchards, the archways, the new ships. The citizens of the mature Soviet state seek cultural understanding. The question that faces the contemporary generation is one of meaning.

Who are we? Who are our parents? And who were our grandparents?

Soloviev's Parable Of Hope

The personalities in *Wild Pigeon* are the uprooted and displaced of the post-war U.S.S.R. It was a difficult time everywhere but in Kazakhstan, in 1946, the situation was especially complex. Thousands of people recently released from Soviet prisons assembled there—not political detainees, but common criminals, thieves, extortionists, frauds of every description. These are the kinds of people that Ivan encounters in his quest for the White One.

Kazakhstan was a place of exile. Stalin's regime, like that of the old Czars, forced the outcasts to stay east of European Russia. Geography, according to the director, also plays a role in the pigeon motif of the film.

"If you were a pigeon fancier, this was the place to be," Soloviev said. "This is the steppe, flat and windswept. All breeds of pigeon converge here, blown by the prevailing winds." [3] The characters in *Wild Pigeon* arrive in Kazakhstan, like the birds, propelled by the crosscurrents of the time.

The film works at many levels. At one level it is the story of a boy's transition to manhood. Ivan's journey towards adulthood originates in his own father's values and attitudes, but he comes to understand those values only in retrospect, through the filter of time, from the distance of the space capsule. Much as the director Gherman journeys in the realm of filial time exploring the characters in his father's short stories, recording the personal side of history from five decades ago, Soloviev takes us back with powerful realism to the period four decades ago when a new era of peace was emerging from the ruin of the war.

"Peace came like a thunderclap," says Ivan in his opening narration as his mind drifts into recollection. We hear a marching band playing. The subtitle *"My Father"* appears on the screen and then another appears: *"This was the 438th day of peace and each day was a holiday."*

The film was shot from a tightly structured three-part script. In the first part Ivan recalls his father, the man's character in the face of adversity, and his relationship with Xenia. In the second part, *"Wild Pigeon,"* Ivan leaves school after a confrontation with his teacher, chases after the White One, and captures her. In the third part, *"Martin's Hideaway,"* the pigeon mafia steals her from him.

The dialogue and the character development in this film have received the careful attention which one might expect of the conventional theater. But at the same time the work is highly filmic in its execution. For all its dramatic structure, the emotive effects of *Wild Pigeon* could not have been accomplished on the traditional stage. The film opens in the space capsule, the camera takes us to earth, we see the town of Aktyubinsk. The camera returns towards the sky. We see the white pigeon in flight. This bifurcated viewpoint, from the universal to the specific, from earth to cosmos, from an engaging and intimate scene to the reminder through voice-over narration and the intrusion of subtitles that all this is a contemporary recollection, re-emerges again and again in the film.

The narration and the dialogue drive the film, but there are parts of it

RISKING ALL FOR THE WHITE ONE: Character Ivan Naidenov, in Soloviev's *Wild Pigeon*, risks his life to capture the elusive White One. (Photo: Courtesy Sovexportfilm)

where the silence and the visuals speak more deeply than the words. Shots of the cosmos are interspersed with images of Xenia's corpse at the morgue, and the speechless faces of her ex-husband Pyotr Petrovich and of Pavel Naidenov here tell the tale. As the second part ends, the film is punctuated again by the subtitled refrain: *"It was the 500th day of peace and still each day was a holiday."*

Sight and sound, dramatic form and cinematic dream interweave in this work, until the tale of Naidenov's boyhood in Kazakhstan transcends itself, becomes a symbolic, detached metaphor, a parable of human hope, of the universal search for meaning.

The prospects of all the characters are bleak. In the wasteland of Aktyubinsk, they search for something to sustain them. Their spirit turns to the mysteriously unattainable, the elusive White One.

"The story is primordial, and contains within itself a symbolic idea which cannot be ignored," Soloviev told me. [4]

"The Naidenovs came from Moscow," says Ivan from the space capsule. "Many people were evacuated to these parts. My mother and I were given shelter by a Kazakh woman. Father wrote to us from the front and we lived from one letter to the next. Then came typhus. I was the first to get sick."

The doctors tell Ivan's mother that he is not long for this world. "Say your goodbyes," they say, but Ivan survives the disease. His mother, infected by her son, dies of it. Pavel Naidenov returns from the front. The father shows his son the mound of earth where the mother lies buried. They paint a blue cross in remembrance.

From his bout with typhus, Ivan has a lock of gray hair. He is known henceforth as Gray. His nickname is not the only one in film that is symbolic. The Chief of Criminal Investigations (Zhous) is the lackey of the black marketeer (Martin). "Zhous" is Russian jailhouse slang for "bribetaker."

In the West Soloviev's motion picture has been released with the title *Wild Pigeon*. The Russian title, however, is *Chuzhaya Belaya i Riaboy (The Strange White and the Speckled)*. The Russian title is intriguing. *Chuzhaya* may mean "wild," but it conveys with it the sense of "strange" or "alien." It means "someone else's, the unattainable." Had Soloviev intended his title to mean "wild" in the sense of "untamed," he could have chosen another substantivized adjective. That word is *dikaya*. There are two prized pigeons in the film: a domesticated Speckled One and the wild strange White One. The Speckled One belongs to Zhous. It hatched curiously from a rotten egg which came from birds given him by his father.

"From the egg there came a half-dead chick. As it grew, Zhous breathed life into it and this pigeon became the forefather of Zhous' Tashkent breed," Ivan recalls.

There are numerous provocative parallelisms in the film. Pavel Naidenov also gives his boy pigeons. Neither son is happy with what he has. Both clamber after the White One. *Wild Pigeon*, like all of Soloviev's works, contains elements of the romantic and the lyrical. We cannot expect from Soloviev the starkness of an Alexei Gherman, but in many ways this film is a turning point for the director. The plot, the soundtrack and the visuals in *Wild Pigeon* form a highly integrated whole. That is Soloviev's trademark. But the characters that he gives us are highly unconventional by Soviet cinema standards. It would have been easy to convert this tale to a milksop nostalgia piece, but to his credit, that is something Soloviev refused to do. He could no more do that than Panfilov could whitewash the life of the writer in the period of stagnation.

Soloviev presents us with highly developed characters but none whom we think of as both morally and socially superior. The boy-hero Gray shares characteristics with the criminal gang he encounters. His father, the wounded war veteran Pavel, is the only character with a clear moral direction, but Pavel is a physical and mental cripple, a stammering idiot sage who lives out his days training unwilling recruits in military procedures.

Gray, although he possesses the forgivable innocence of a child, is as ruthless and as daring as the pigeon mafia.

Zhous, Martin and the boys, for all their corruption, aspire to the spiritual in their quest for the White One. Risking his life, hanging from a steep and slippery roof, Gray captures the White One. Zhous, Martin and the rest of the underworld are hot on his heels. They steal her from him.

In a battle of wits with the pigeon-mafia godfather, Martin, the pugnacious Gray reclaims her. Martin has set a wolf trap to snare the boy, but the scoundrel gets caught in it himself.

Gray couldn't care less. He can only think of the pigeon. "Here you are, my clever one, my indescribable beauty. Look at you. You're as white as snow," he says as Martin moans in the background.

The crippled Pavel must plead with his son to help release Martin from the trap. The boy shows no mercy. He would leave him there.

Gray eventually releases Martin, but the boy will not possess the White One. In the final scene, taking a step that brings him one step closer to maturity, he sets her free to the wind. She is *chuzhaya*. He returns her where she belongs.

The boy too will have a future. He too will soar above mankind. We hear the clock ticking in the capsule and the credits flash before us.

The Imperfect Hero

Gleb Panfilov's co-writer Alexander Chervinsky discussed with me the reasons that *Theme* had been banned. Yes, he said, the portrayal of the Jewish gravedigger-writer who wants to emigrate may have helped to send the film to cold storage. Emigrants were regarded as traitors. You weren't supposed to talk to those kinds of people.

Such forbidden subject matter was not however the primary cause of the film's exile to the deep freeze, Chervinsky felt. The real problem was the character of the hero of the film. Kim Yesenin is not a hero at all in the traditional conception. A writer should be a leader. His art should inspire. He should be the conscience of the people. Yesenin is none of these things.

"Yesenin has achieved high status," said Chervinsky. "He is an official writer, but inside he doesn't know why he exists. He goes to a medieval town to find, as he calls it, some replenishment. He is in search of some positive ideal, but what he sees, what he finds instead, is spiritual schism and uncertainty. This central image of the writer was most probably the main reason for the film being shelved." [5]

Yesenin's life is one of confusion and lack of commitment. In contrast to the gravedigger Andrei, who for the sake of truth would cut himself off from homeland, lover and art itself, Yesenin struggles with the idea of artistic compromise, but tries to find some balance. He knows the truth, but he does not wish to face it. Alone in his car, he talks to himself. As he looks in the rear-view mirror, his own empty eyes look back at him and he cringes.

Outside the cottage where the provincial scribes and their guests from Moscow gather for an evening soiree, the warm light of the windows beckons magnetically in soft focus through the winter air. Inside turmoil prevails.

Kim is infatuated with the mueum guide/biographer, Sasha. Like a 19th century heroine, her intellect embodies all that is noble in Russian culture. Yet Sasha, whose every glance and every gesture appears to invite hope and inward peace, pronounces him spiritually dead.

The playwright responds with a tantrum. He seizes Pashchin's typewriter and smashes it to the floor.

Sasha treats Kim's outburst as if it were the action of a spoiled child. He is not beyond redemption, she feels. She has issued him a challenge. The flame of art once burned in him. A spark remains. She hopes to rekindle it. She invites him to go with her to the grave of the poet Chizhikov. At the gravesite, Yesenin is reborn. He determines that he will write again truthfully, that he will be whole. Later, however, his determination falters as he witnesses Andrei's parting with Sasha.

Kim goes to Sasha's apartment and, hiding behind her refrigerator, secretly overhears her telling the poet that a writer cut off from his country is also dead. Sobbing, she begs Andrei not to go. Andrei, angry and despairing, strikes Sasha, knocking her to the floor, and then leaves. Kim steps over her unconscious body planning to make his escape back to the city. He repents of course. Like a moth to the light, he is drawn back to her, back to the phone booth where he meets his symbolic end and where his Volga automobile burns in an eerie conflagration behind him. In the darkness, the burning car illuminates the snowbound land and we hear the voice of a young woman humming a lament. The car is symbolically both a funeral pyre and a flame of hope—a phoenix rising.

The Song of Prince Igor's Campaign also comes to a climax (though not a conclusion) with a lament. Igor's wife wails from the walls of the town of Putivl bemoaning her mate's capture by the Polovtsy. The conclusion of the poem is a chant of praise to the national spirit, a prayer for the unification of the motherland which has its origins in the liturgy of the Byzantine sacred oratory. The poet Bayan's prayer is that the land divided by the petty squabbles of its princes shall be one.

Theme is a song of praise and lament for the spirit of Russian literature and the community of writers. Its visual liturgy seeks the reunification of literary purpose and practice which has been torn asunder by the demands of the state. Perhaps the release of Panfilov's film portends such a future for Soviet artists. Perhaps in glasnost and perestroika may be found the beginning of the second golden age of Soviet cinema, a time like the first, when national and artistic goals were synonymous.

Futility is always the dilemma of artists who do not make choices based on creative honesty. The protagonist of *Theme* writes plays for Komsomols much as the playwrights of the American electronic theater may be said to make plays for soap merchants. Kim has the same surname as the illustrious Russian poet Sergei Yesenin—a fact that was not lost on Soviet audiences or the censors who relegated the film to the deep freeze. In the film we are told that Kim was born on the same day that Sergei died. Disenchanted, eight years after the revolution, Yesenin, like Mayakovsky, committed suicide. His last statement was a poem written in his own blood. A year before his death, he wrote:

> I all accept—just as it is I take it.
> And I'm prepared to tread the beaten field,
> To May, October dedicate my spirit,
> But only my sweet lyre I will not yield. [6]

Vladimir Mayakovsky and Sergei Yesenin were literary antitheses. Mayakovsky was prepared, as he said, for the sake of the Party, to set

THEME: In Gleb Panfilov's *Theme* the only true artist is a dead one—Alexander Yegorovich Chizhikov (Chizhik). Here, hero and heroine of the film, Kim Yesenin and the woman with whom he is infatuated, Sasha, visit the poet's gravesite. (Photo: Courtesy Sovexportfilm)

his heel "on the throat of his own song." Mayakovsky's poems march to the beat of the revolutionary comrades. Yesenin is the romantic lyricist out of step with his time who will not give up his lyre. Then as now the dichotomy of focus pervades the Soviet literary and artistic environment. For a time the rationalist, objective voices dominate, and then the subjective and the lyrical ones re-emerge as they have in the glasnost cinema.

The imperfect hero, the distanced artistic viewpoint of the new cinema, was not readily accepted by the old guard who controlled Goskino. The film board could and did prevent the distribution of the films, but it could not prevent dedicated artists from producing their controversial works. Now that a new generation is assuming control in Soviet society, the work of Gherman and Panfilov and others is being declassified and it has gone from cultural banishment to prize-winning success at international festivals.

My Friend Ivan Lapshin won the Bronze Leopard at the Locarno Festival in 1986. That same year *Wild Pigeon* received the Special Grand Prix of the Jury in Venice. *Theme* took the Golden Bear at Berlin in 1987. How well filmmakers will wear the mantle of state acceptance, however, remains to be seen. Alexei Gherman, like Sartre, sees art as an act of commitment: to be a director one must have a stance, an "authenticity," a *pozitsia*.

"As I see it, without a stance, one cannot be a real authentic contemporary director," Gherman told the American film scholar Donna Turkish Seifer in a video-taped interview in Moscow. "In our country to a very great degree an authentic film director is in a 'militant' position. We have, as you do, an enormous number of director-waiters. This is the type that carries a tray and will bring you anything you want. And there is a number of directors who possess a set of principles in cinema as in life. They defend these principles. So in my opinion, a contemporary film director is a director who first and foremost has a stance . . . a stance in art, a stance in politics, a stance in everything."

How well will Gherman adapt to the new glasnost freedoms?

"Now that everything is permitted, where should I start? God only knows," the director says. "You can do this, and this, and this. It is a very difficult question when all is permitted. It turns out that art sometimes comes out better when it is forbidden."

Gherman and Panfilov have been only moderately productive as directors. Since co-directing his first movie in 1968, Gherman has made three films independently. Over the same time period, Panfilov has directed seven. Panfilov divides his time between cinema and theater. Gherman has been occupying himself writing scripts for others. At the time of the interview, it was uncertain when, if ever, he would direct another film. Frankly, he makes more money writing scripts.

"We have a saying in Russia," he told Seifer. "It is better to be rich and healthy, than sick and poor."[7]

There is some inconsistency in his current endeavors and his sophisticated attitude toward the role of the director, but he says: "Man is weak . . . I'm confused. I don't know what to do."[8]

Whatever the future holds for the radical innovators of the new artform, one thing is certain: the art of cinematic introspection and its imperfect hero are here to stay. Pavel Naidenov, the father of the protagonist in *Wild Pigeon,* provides some clues to the origins of the new hero.

To the military recruits that Pavel instructs, his stuttering speech and awkward mannerisms are a joke. For them the war is over. They taunt him, they mimic him and while he is in a washroom cubicle, they almost kill him with a gas grenade. Even Ivan's school teacher unwittingly abuses Pavel.

In a classroom scene, the teacher gives a literature lesson on the prerevolutionary writer Turgenev while outside Pavel's stammering voice is heard giving directions in the use of machine guns and automatic pistols.

> **Teacher:** Here we are, boys. The topic is an interesting and contemporary one. Remember that we will make a comparison. In our present-day life, there are no superfluous people as you well know and there can be none. Therefore, think carefully and then without further thought, plunge bravely into a comparison with the era of Czar Nicholas I. Pay attention to your grammar, boys. Write, write, don't lose any time.
> **Pavel:** Take for example the German Schmeizer (breaks into a stutter) Mmmmmmmmmmm. Ech. Ech.
> **Teacher:** (looking out the window as the boys are writing) Really unbearable, isn't it? (imitates Pavel) Ech . . . Ech . . . There you have it, boys: the great and glorious Russian language! . . . (Ivan gets up to leave.) Naidenov! Naidenov! What's the matter with you? Were you offended?
> **Ivan:** Why should I be offended? That my father didn't die. That he only suffered a concussion. He is a shell-shocked invalid. Don't you understand that? He has paid his dues and he has a medical certificate to prove his injuries. Why do you fill people's minds with such nonsense? Isn't he the superfluous man?

The superfluous heroes of 19th century Russian literature, such as

Turgenev's Rudin in the novel of the same name, are defeated, rejected characters, slightly ridiculous, destined to lives of unrealized potential. Drawn from the ranks of the liberal intelligentsia, they were despised by officials and distrusted by larger society.

The superfluous hero was a dreamer. He had strong moral views, as Pavel does, but was fated to failure. Such a hero in the socialist-realist tradition was anathema, for such men stand aside from the dogma of their time and refuse to be integrated into the common ethos. In the monolithic state, where all conflicts have been resolved and alienation has been abolished, as Ivan's teacher proclaims: "There are no superfluous people, and there can be none."

Ivan's father shares many characteristics with the 19th century hero. Prior to the war he had been a talented artist, a member of the creative intelligentsia. Like many pre-revolutionary literary figures he is in love with a beautiful yet unobtainable woman. He loves Xenia Nikolaevna. He would do anything for her, but he will not let himself become involved. It wouldn't be right. He tries instead to re-unite her with her estranged husband, the pianist-composer and former friend of Rachmaninov, Pyotr Petrovich. Pavel has a strong moral outlook and he is not afraid to express it. He stands as foil to the corruption and degradation that he finds around him.

After his recruits have gassed him, breathing heavily, breaking into coughing fits, he tells his son of a close encounter he had with the authorities in Birobidjan. Birobidjan is an Oblast, a province in the eastern limits of Siberia, which was created by Stalin for the Jews. A Birobidjanian saves Pavel from false arrest by the police.

"He thought it was curtains for me," Pavel recalls. "And then he said: 'To hell with it. It only looks like curtains because there are a lot of them. They have the power, but that's nonsense.'"

"They are . . . ," says Pavel making a lewd gesture signifying contempt. "And we are . . . ," he says giving the thumbs up sign. "Remember that, Ivan. Your world is your pigeon coop. You believe in it. That is your pigeon happiness, but life, that is something else."

In the broader literal connotation of the word, if not in the classical literary sense, all the characters in *Wild Pigeon* and similarly in *Theme* and in *My Friend Ivan Lapshin* can be regarded as superfluous. They are portrayed on the periphery of society. Remote, sparsely populated settlements are their stage. Their individual actions and thoughts are insignificant in the larger arena. They are atoms of history, not its heroes, but precisely because they stand in contrast to the mono-heroes that have dominated Soviet art since the 1930s, they attain a significance that cannot be overlooked. The positive hero had the answers. For him there was no need for reflection.

Soviet writer and journalist Ilya Ehrenburg spoke with a young female lab assistant who, when the first sputnik was launched, asked on an open-line show: "We have our engineers of human souls, but where are our sputniks of the human heart?" The woman's question launched the Thaw debate.

The works of Soloviev and Gherman and Panfilov are for the glasnost cinema such "sputniks of the heart."

4 • *Directors of Glasnost:*
A Filmography

Vadim Abdrashitov

Stop Potapov (1974)
A Word for the Defense (1977) (w/ Alexander Mindadze)
The Change/ The Turn (1979)
The Fox Hunt/ Fox-Hunting (1980)
A Train Has Stopped (1982)
Parade of Planets (1984)
Plumbum, or A Dangerous Game (1986)
The Manservant/ The Servant (a fable) (1989)

Abdrashitov, an "army brat" and former engineer, applied to VGIK three times before being admitted by Romm. His first film, a satire, was an instant hit and showed a keen eye for social problems and everyday petty dramas.

In 1977, the intense Abdrashitov teamed up with scriptwriter Alexander Mindadze, son of the famous scriptwriter Anatoli Grebnev, to collaborate on all subsequent films. They have become the leading exponents of the rationalist trend in Soviet cinema, specializing in pictures that provoke viewers by exposing public and social problems.

Structurally, their works provide clear-cut plots with contrasting parallelism and well-delineated characters. Each film uncovers a moral conflict complemented by terse, understated camera techniques which emphasize subtle nuances and half-tones. The filmmakers' mastery of technique helps their work to avoid being labelled essayist.

The Fox Hunt, for example, is a metaphor for finding one's own way through the maze of contemporary social conditions and life. The ancient art of the tracking game is replaced by a modern sport, where players wear head-sets and follow signals from hidden transmitters.

After the canny, champion fox-hunter is assaulted by hoodlums, he experiences a catharsis and visits one of his attackers in a corrective labor camp, hoping to change the young man's outlook.

The Change describes a decent, intellectual married couple who knock down an old woman while rounding a turn in their car. Though technically not guilty, they are scared and attempt to bribe witnesses, causing a turn or change in their lives.

A Train Has Stopped is also realism with a down-to-earth, believable plot. An investigator and a journalist sent to the scene of a train crash are impeded in their inquiries by the authorities and the local people, even by the widow of the heroic driver of a faulty locomotive who saved the passengers' lives.

"Why not whitewash the whole report if nobody cares," the outsiders ask themselves.

Sharing a cramped hotel room, but alienated from each other, the strangers decide it is their duty to tell their independent versions of the truth. Public opinion prevails, covering up the incident with a plausible though indecisive explanation. The riddle behind the crash has many answers, but Abdrashitov, who studied Hitchcock, provokes his audience, then leaves them in suspense.

Parade of Planets is his most alienating picture. According to the director, it was a shift in direction for him. He used as a model, he says, the themes and conventions of modern Latin-American fiction. The film's unexpected twists reflect this influence. It borrows an ever-extending metaphor: planets lining up to one side of the sun in a threatening "parade" along with stars and timeless, transcendental truths. These truths, however, cannot guide the individual or influence his normal life. The heroes who are symbolically "killed" in battle maneuvres are sent home and journey through a fantastic city of women, an enchanted island and a mysterious senior citizens' residence. Each person that they meet reminds them to believe in their self-worth and to change, for they are needed by society and their loved ones. Unable to accept this simple truth or sift reality from delirium, they return home forgetting everything, including those opportunities that fate had put before them.

Although it could be said that some of Abdrashitov's and Mindadze's films revive socialist-realist canons of heroism, duty and worth to society, they probe the marginal, unglamorous reaches of Soviet life, avoid pat optimism and show a brutal struggle of the soul based on individual conscience. Their tough approach to problems is palpable, and more realist than socialist. This is borne out by the contrasting reviews their films receive.

Stormy debates rage over *Plumbum*. Is Ruslan Chutko a typical schoolboy found in almost every school, or an invented test-tube monster? Is he an adolescent needed by perestroika or the antithesis, a romanticized fascist? Clearly, Abdrashitov and Mindadze's ambitious, cruel and bitter soul-searching leads to a cerebral *pozitsia* that defines them as social pathfinders in contemporary Soviet film.

(For more on *Plumbum*, see Chapter 2.)

Tengiz Abuladze

*The State Ensemble of Georgian Folkdance
and Our Palace (1954)* (doc. w/Revaz Chkheidze)
Magdana's Lurdzha (Donkey) (1955) (w/ Revaz Chkheidze)
Strange Children/ Other People's Children (1958)
Me, My Grandmother, Iliko and Illarion (1963)
The Svanski Sketches (1965)
The Plea/ Prayer/ Supplication (1968)
The Open-Air Museum/Daghestan (TV) *(1972)*
A Necklace for My Beloved (1973)
Wishing Tree (1977)
Repentance (1986)

It took four years, the personal backing of Foreign Minister Eduard Shevardnadze, the 27th CPSU Congress, the 5th SFU Congress, and the strongest appeals from the Conflict Committee to obtain release for Abuladze's *Repentance*. Its liberation from bureaucratic captivity signalled the Age of Perestroika. This cornerstone of glasnost was shot at the behest of Gruzia Telefilm, but was quickly removed from TV. Georgian police rounded up stray videotapes and those who had them.

Although he is a rationalist like Abdrashitov, Abuladze is also a film-poet who breaks with socialist-realist traditions, as do fellow Georgian Georgi Shengelaya and Armenian director Sergei Paradjanov.

Abuladze and Chkheidze shared the Cannes Grand Prix when they were in their early 30s for the 1955 short film, *Magdana's Lurdzha*. The international attention given to the film was symbolic for Soviet Cinema—a sign that the decade of dogmatism, otherwise known as the period of Non-Cinema (mid-40s to the beginning of the 50s), was coming to an end. This, their first (and last) short feature together, was a lyrical, sad film about the hard lot of a group of Georgian peasants and their donkey.

While Abuladze favored lyricism, he soon adopted an ascetic, almost documentary style resembling Italian neorealism, yet quite distinct from it because the melodramatic scenarios were presented as parables.

In his film *Strange Children*, a young woman marries a good-for-nothing widower who is not only a burden himself, but leaves her with his two children to bring up as best she can. In this plain story the director discovers a law of life: the weak are always at the mercy of the impudent and powerful. It is not tyrants alone who make gentle innocent people suffer. The suffering may come from the tragic confusion of the world, as it does in his next film, *Me, My Grandmother, Iliko and Illarion*, which shows inhabitants of a mountain village receiving death certificates from the front. Despite its melancholy theme, the parable is handled with great humor, gentle sarcasm and a touch of the grotesque.

The turning point in Abuladze's opus came not with a change in his central theme of injustice, but with a change of historical and philosophical perspective. Long before glasnost he claimed the right to memory on the behalf of contemporary culture.

"Abuladze could no longer look at history directly like gazing at the sun,"[1] *Repentance* scriptwriter Rezo Kveselava told me. He chose instead historical abstraction, preferring visual metaphor to his earlier neorealism. The director's attitude toward history, to cultural and spiritual values found its fruition in the parable-film-narrative. Gruziafilm has an undisputed claim as the epicenter of this unique genre.

Repentance is the third film in Abuladze's definitive trilogy, which includes his 1968 work *The Plea* and his 1977 film *The Wishing Tree*. Symbolically, the three films are bound by the subject of faith. *The Plea* preserves the mythological Vazha Pshavela's folk-heroic saga of an outcast warrior who defies ancient law by not cutting off the hand of a slain enemy. The tribal thirst for vengeance calls for the pursuit of two victims to undo the curse. In addition, an innocent maiden (a beautiful allegorical figure of Justice) must be sacrificed. The cycle of evil which continues to the present day is parodied with Chaplinesque humor as officials dressed in tuxedos and bowler hats are shown digging graves.

The sequel, *Wishing Tree*, is a free-filming of G. Leonidze's memoirs—prose lightened with poetry—portraying the mores and manners of a turn-of-the-century Georgian village. *Wishing Tree*, liberally spiced with humor, pokes fun at superstition. The film is full of comical characters—a buxom maid-of-easy-virtue, an oversized teenager who doesn't know his own strength, a libidinal, avaricious priest and an anarchist who listens for trains—all searching for a magical tree of happiness.

"I hear the Revolution coming," the anarchist says, as he puts his ear to the track.

Wishing Tree is also a film about brutal customs. A young girl who is "sold" into a pre-arranged marriage and who is magnificent in her wretchedness is publicly stoned to death when she displays her pure feelings for her true lover. Her affections have threatened the authority

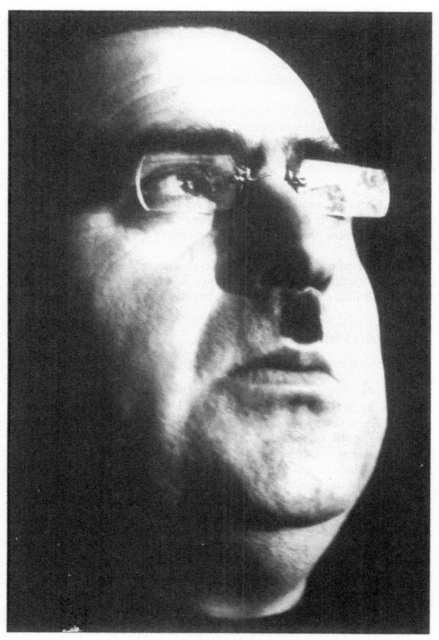

VARLAM, the central figure of Tengiz Abuladze's *Repentance*, is a pudgy backslapper who wears Beria-style glasses and a Hitler moustache. (Photo: Courtesy Sovexportfilm)

of her mother-in-law and of the rich man who arranged the wedding. When she dies, credulous villagers believe her spirit takes the form of a "wishing tree" which grows nearby.

Repentance completes the trilogy. Again the focus is the lack of rights for the weak and the injustice of the powerful, but here an entire people is shown as the victim.

Striving for universality, Abuladze scrupulously avoids specific references to Georgia, and generalizes the central figure of Varlam. *Repentance* is more than a mere exposure of the Stalin cult. Absurdist humor, slapstick and caricature contribute to his generalized view of Any Tyrant.

Varlam is a pudgy backslapper with a Hitler moustache. On his inaugeration day he order his cronies to read impromptu speaches when it starts to rain. The downpour, the viewer discovers, is from a broken water main below the podium which workers are furiously trying to fix.

The entire trilogy is framed in a prayer and throughout the concepts of Christian faith emerge and re-emerge. Even the most grotesque and tragic of Abuladze's films have divine beauty. (See also Chapter 1.)

Alexander Askoldov

Commissar (1967)

Askoldov, a director of the 1960s, chose a Jewish theme, although he was not of Jewish heritage himself. He is the son of a political Commissar who was arrested in the '30s purges. Goskino fired Askoldov for "incompetence."

Commissar was hidden by Askoldov's wife for 20 years until it made an unscheduled, virtually clandestine appearance at the 1987 Moscow International Film Festival. Its screening was prompted by loud requests from American guests, and it has since reached wider audiences in both the East and West. The SFU Conflict Committee aided in its release.

Commissar represents a significant reworking of the Vasili Grossman story of the early '30s: *It Happened in Berdichev*. The film is set in the southern Ukraine town of Berdichev during the civil war; its protagonist is a stout, ruthless woman who metes out revolutionary justice to Red Army deserters.

"The Revolution protects itself," she says.

Ironically, she is left behind by her comrades and billeted with poor Jewish townsfolk when it is discovered that she is six months pregnant. The head of the household, a tinker, is as loudly disgusted by her presence as she is by his.

"They think I'm a Rothschild," he says.

She rejoins her comrades, abandoning her child to the family, who wish that revolutions could be more "humane."

The mixed lyrical-epic style is in the Eisenstein/Dovzhenko tradition and the film employs some unusual montage sequences, such as a flash-forward to the Holocaust, while the beautiful musical soundtrack consists of Russian and Jewish lullabies. Askoldov's overt Jewish sympathy, sexual portrayal of Commissar Klavdia and the religious focus symbolized by a "trinity" of churches (Synagogue, Orthodox and Catholic) eclipse in importance the Bolshevik revolutionary zeal. Aesthetically, *Commissar* is a masterpiece. Politically, it is one of the most controversial movies in the history of Soviet Film.

Rolan Bykov

> *Seven Nannies (1962)*
> (a feature comedy, with Nikolai Orlov)
> *Summer's Over (1964)* (comedy, with Nikolai Orlov)
> *Oh How It Hurts-66 (1964)* (musical)
> *Caution! Turtle!/ Attention, Tortoise! (1970)*
> *The Telegram (1972)*
> *A Car, a Violin and a Dog Named Spot (1975)*
> (children's film)
> *The Nose* (TV) *(1977)*
> *The Wedding Gift (1983)* (w/ Rezo Esadze)
> *Scarecrow (1984)*

Bykov has made several children's movies, but *Scarecrow*, an officially criticized film, re-creates a microcosm of Stalinist repression in a village school where sadistic students ostracize a shy pupil and her innocent grandfather. In the film, a 12-year-old girl wants to be called Iron Girl, a metaphorical reference to Stalin, The Man of Steel. It is a model for anti-Stalinist films and films about teenagers that follow, such as Abdrashitov's *Plumbum, or A Dangerous Game*. *Scarecrow*, like Leida Laius' *Games for Teenagers*, drew attention from parent/teacher associations, special screenings and controversy in the press.

Director Bykov is also a prolific actor, appearing in several shelved films such as Askoldov's *Commissar* and Gherman's *Trial on the Road*. He plays the scientist Larsen in Lopushansky's *Letters from a Dead Man*. In Gherman's film he is the officer who places trust in a soldier whom others call a traitor, while in Askoldov's movie he plays the Jewish patriarch. Bykov has directed difficult films and performed in demanding roles. He has been head of a new youth studio which is financially subordinate to Mosfilm, but creatively independent. Its first offering was Georgi Gavrilov's hybrid documentary feature *Confession: A Chronicle of Alienation*, which examined the life of a young Soviet drug addict.

Grigori Chukhrai

The Forty-First (1956)
Ballad of a Soldier (1959)
Clear Sky (1961)
Once Upon a Time Lived an Old Man and
  an Old Woman (1965)
Memory (1971)
The Quagmire/ An Untypical Story (1977)
Life Is Marvellous (1980) (Italian co-production)
I'll Teach You to Dream (1985)

From 1965-75 Chukhrai headed the Mosfilm Experimental Studio and its television counterpart ETO. He taught at VGIK between 1966-71 and has served as a secretary at SFU since 1965. In this capacity he has been at the forefront of recent cinema reforms. His talented son, Pavel Chukhrai, is now also directing movies.

Film educator Mikhail Romm regarded Chukhrai as a protégé, helping the ex-paratrooper enter VGIK and work on projects while he convalesced from the after-effects of heavy wounds received in the war. In 1953 Chukhrai assisted Romm in making *Admiral Ushakov*.

The Forty-First, his directorial debut, is a remarkably apolitical story of two lovers on opposite sides of the revolution and the tragic death of the man who, while serving with the White forces, is killed by the woman he loves.

His second picture, *Ballad of a Soldier*, much better known in the West, was hailed in America by *Time* magazine in early 1961 as "the best Russian movie made since World War II." [2] More to the point, however, this film could be accused of giving socialist realism a good name, since it features a typical positive hero, Alyosha, who for his bravery is given a pass to see his mother. He then experiences innocent love before returning to the front to die.

In *Ballad of a Soldier*, the viewer's attention is skilfully diverted away from the skeletal plot by the film's technique, mostly lyrical, which stresses filial and first love. The technical peculiarities of the film (soft focus, superimpositions, musical score, etc.) propel the love plot. In this respect, this movie together with Mikhail Kalatozov's *The Cranes Are Flying (1958)* was a harbinger of the Thaw in cinema.

Russians adore Chukhrai's film, and I was told by American film scholar Louis Menashe that he saw a re-enactment of the closing scene on a sports telecast in Moscow. To his surprise, during the intermission an Army truck pulled up inside the stadium, "Alyosha" jumped out, his "mother" dashed towards him, and they embraced in center field.

The 1961 feature, *Clear Sky* describes a Soviet pilot who is captured by the Fascists and who returns to his homeland to face suspicion and distrust. It is one of the earliest films of the Thaw period to explore anti-Stalinist sentiment with no holds barred. Because of its directness, Rezo Kveselava, the scriptwriter of Abuladze's *Repentance,* considers *Clear Sky* to be a forerunner of his film.

Memory recalls the Battle of Stalingrad through reminiscences, and *Quagmire,* which was long withheld from circulation, tells a mother's story of how she hid her son from conscription.

Georgi Danelia

Also People (1959)
Seryozha (1960) (w/ Igor Talankin)
The Way to the Harbor (1962)
I Walk in Moscow/ Walking the Streets of Moscow (1963)
Thirty-Three/ 33 (1965)
Don't Grieve! (1969)
Hopelessly Lost (1972)
Afonya (1975)
Mimino (1977)
Autumn Marathon (A Sad Comedy) (1979)
Tears Dripped/ Tears Are Falling (1983)
Kin-Dza-Dza (1986)

Danelia, another Romm student who is Georgian but works at Mosfilm, specializes in comedy. With the exception of his first three films—*Also People* (an excerpt from Tolstoy's *War and Peace*), *Seryozha* (Vera Panova's story about a child, same title) and the psychological drama *The Way to the Harbor*—all are films d'auteur, incorporating lyricism, the grotesque, satire, tragicomedy, irony and self-irony. In all of them there is a touch of joy and sadness, as in *Autumn Marathon (A Sad Comedy),* a love film about a man in mid-life crisis caught up in a comical urban "rat race."

In search of the simplicity that only great artists achieve, Danelia is a perfectionist, like Charles Chaplin or Woody Allen, who agonizes for months reworking good scenes. Like Alfred Hitchcock, he makes cameo appearances in all his movies. Danelia's fleeting cameo appearance as a one-eyed SS-man in a TV program undoubtedly would amuse Allen. Such scenes as these, however, are punctuation marks to tantalizing understatement. As a result, Danelia's films have mystery and his satirical science-fiction comedy *Kin-Dza-Dza* could be compared to Allen's *Sleeper*.

Like Woody Allen, Danelia takes on the role of an omniscient, universal sage. In outer space, just as on earth or in the future, you always find one humanoid ill-treating another. Allen's hero pretends to be a robot butler to avoid abuse; Danelia's earthling heroes masquerade as a comedian and a musician. Allen steals the nose of the dictator he is cloning and runs it over with a steamroller to stop the evil. Danelia kindheartedly turns the depraved, corrupt souls from the planet Kin-Dza-Dza into cactii, so they should purify themselves through meditation in a valley of flowers. Both directors tolerate no lies and make strong moral statements about contemporary society, with its corruption, hedonism and tyranny. They also share Chaplin's wise conviction that simplicity is truth and seek this simplicity in humans, punishing the most despicable of them.

To underscore his point, Danelia invented a special language for his picture called *patsak-chatlan*, providing the viewer with a glossary to this alien tongue. At first he wanted to call his film *Coo*, a Kin-Dza-Dzian interjection which varies in intonation to signify hostile or friendly intentions. The absurd word *coo* symbolizes universal human contact, imploring us to look at ourselves. Danelia clearly declares his love for us, no matter how confused we may be, but adds the warning that we ourselves pose our kind the greatest threat.

A former architect like Eisenstein, Danelia also designed all of the details of his set, from catacombs and dugouts to futuristic palaces, space vehicles and clothes. The universe he creates is a high-tech/low-tech wilderness, a garbage-heap worthy of George Miller's *Mad Max, Road Warrior* and *Beyond the Thunderdome*.

In the opening scene of *Kin-Dza-Dza*, a Moscow construction superintendent and a teenager take pity on a hobo and press a button on his miniature switchboard only to find themselves transported to his strange planet. They are greeted by two dishevelled men who emerge from a spaceship and coo at them. The naive Moscovites first marvel at their primitive-looking hosts, their grimy, beat-up vehicle, their stupid gestures and dearth of language. Later, they realize that they are captives of slavers who put bells on their noses and force them to learn their rich but profane tongue. The pair kowtow, sing and dance to please their alien masters without success until one of the Moscovites lights a match.

Unknown to the protagonists, matches have become the medium of exchange (hard currency) of the future, although of course they have no intrinsic value. Schooled in profanity and rude treatment, and now in possession of enormous "wealth," they realize the whole planet turns on interpersonal abuse. They have found the secret of success and begin to emulate the black-marketeers who control the planet. The film ends when they return to Moscow wondering if anyone will recognize them.

The satire is not lost on Moscow audiences who recollect a patently false rumor circulated in the '60's that there would be a shortage of matches in the city (which caused a real shortage to occur) and that this major item of export to the West in the '60s was captioned by a proud logo which proclaimed "the whole world uses Soviet matches." The folk humor of the day ridiculed it:

Chas trenia,	Rub and rub an hour,
Chas terpenia,	An hour we play the game.
Snachala von'	First the stench of sulphur,
Potom ogon'	And finally the flame.

Obviously several levels of satire operate in Danelia's film. On at least one of these levels he portrays the absurdity of the Soviet black market where the obsession with materialism approaches the grotesque. On another, he suggests the impotence of the State to deliver the most basic commodities which results in the devastation of values. In the uncompromising vocabulary of perestroika and glasnost, *Kin-Dza-Dza* is an intriguing metaphor for both.

Nana Djordjadze

Robinsonada / My English Grandfather (1987)

Djordjadze's Gruziafilm production, *My English Grandfather,* is based on a script by her husband, Georgian director Irakli Kvirikadze, who made another controversial movie called *The Swimmer* in 1982. *My English Grandfather* is a treat for Western viewers as the protagonist speaks English while Russian viewers are provided with subtitles for his dialogue. For Soviet audiences, it restores a little-known episode of Georgian history.

Set in the revolution, the story is about Christopher Hughes, the English grandfather, who as a young man comes to the Georgian village of Sio in 1920 to build a link to the London-Delhi telegraph line. There he meets Anna, the sister of the Commune Chairman, Nestor. The feisty Christopher and Nestor are soulmates until they quarrel over politics and come to blows in a hilarious boxing match. Anna is henceforth for-

MY ENGLISH GRANDFATHER: Like Robinson Crusoe, marooned on an island, Christopher Hughes (the English Grandfather) defends what he declares is British territory, the three yards of land around the poles of the London-Delhi telegraph line. In order not to set foot on foreign soil, he rides a donkey. (Photo: Courtesy Sovexportfilm)

bidden to see the Englishman, whom Nestor exiled from the village, yet she visits her beloved every day.

Hughes, who declares that Britain has title to three yards of land around each telegraph pole on the London-Delhi line, insists on protecting "British territory." Like Robinson Crusoe, he inhabits one of these "islands" himself. So as not to "set foot" on the foreign soil from which he is banished, he rides into town on a donkey.

One day Nestor decides to make up with his "relative" and comes to see Hughes in his "England," but is shot in the back by a local landlord who avenges himself on the Communist foe. Hughes, who rushes up to the body, is also killed. Anna witnesses the death of her lover and brother, but her lover is never mentioned again. Only his memory is cherished by her and the family, and his spirit and likeness are preserved in the English-speaking grandson, a composer, to whom Anna's and Hughes' story is finally told.

The retro-aspect of the picture is captured in interviews with an old woman (Anna) and in faded sepia photographs of old Georgia, but the film's point of view, as imagined through the eyes of Hughes' grandson, is overwhelmingly modern. A humorous twist in the story is that the grandson now speaks English with a distinctly American accent, though he is played by the same actor as Hughes. Djordjadze's film is a vivid and tender restoration of a historical moment, the reclamation of which is made possible through glasnost.

Alexei Gherman

Workers' Quarters (1965)
The Seventh Companion/ Sputnik (1968) (w/ Grigori
   Aronov)
Trial on the Road/ Checkpoint (1971)
Twenty Days without War (1977)
My Friend Ivan Lapshin (1984)

Gherman's creations are among the most acclaimed revelations of recently unshelved Soviet films. It is almost impossible not to agree with Ian Christie, critic of the 1987 London Film Festival, who writes: "History was never like this in Soviet cinema before, except perhaps in Tarkovsky's *Mirror*, which shares with *Ivan Lapshin* an autobiographical thread and laconic portrayal of everyday life in the Stalin era."[3]

Gherman's first significant movie, *Seventh Companion*, was co-authored with Grigori Aronov and is an adaption of a Boris Lavrenev short story. His next three films are also based on stories (his father

Yuri's, and Konstantin Simonov's) but they are nevertheless his own creations and bear his personal stamp. Thematically and structurally they comprise a historical trilogy of the '30s and '40s that may be viewed in any order, as if one were travelling in Wells' Time Machine.

To ensure authenticity, Gherman rummaged through documents and archival photos which he clipped to a board, and scoured second-hand shops for genuine articles, before making each movie or episode. He does not order reality because he hates false cinema with "the furbished buttons." He mocks this in the figure of a military consultant on a movie set (in *Twenty Days without War*) who insists "soldiers' buttons must glitter." On this point Gherman was apparently corrected by a war vet who reportedly said: "We wanted to shine them for photos to show we were proud." [4]

Gherman not only creates the true atmosphere of the '30s and '40s, but exudes a warm attitude toward this period and its people with a sense of filial piety and filial time. With his time-machine camera he brings them to us just as easily as he took his father's typewriter and globe to his set (in *Ivan Lapshin*). He does not restore the past as retro-filmmakers do, but makes it part of a living memory, like the cameraman who photographs his or her own shadow.

Trial on the Road, based on Yuri Gherman's story *Operation Happy New Year,* concerns the forced collaborator Lazarev (the Biblical Lazarus raised from the dead), who offers, as a last act of conscience, to sacrifice his life by helping to destroy a Nazi base. Commander Bolshakov (Colonel "Big") wants to shoot him, but Captain Lokotkov (the "Right-Hand-Man") wisely disagrees. They quarrel bitterly, but Lazarev completes the mission and dies heroically, confirming Lokotkov's trust. The captain and the colonel don't meet again until the final days of war when Bolshakov sees Lokotkov pushing a mired truck.

"I'll write the Field-Marshal about you," he shouts, then adds, "Our cannon pound Berlin and [he] is still a captain."

In Gherman's lens all three men are peripheral and integral to history. In *Twenty Days without War,* a correspondent, Major Lopatin (the hero of several Simonov stories) is sent far from the front to report on the situation back home and to assist in making a war movie. He discovers people who rise above hardship and tragedy like the woman who applies makeup to pose for a picture while a bomb explodes behind her, destroying a wall. He sees the whole country stand up behind a shabbily dressed orchestra of old men and women tormented with hunger who lift their spirit in national song. But he also sees through the lies about war which are presented to them by officials. When he returns to the front lines the film ends with the words: "It was a long, long way to Berlin." The distancing technique, via peripheral camera perspectives and fragmented points-of-view, provides an unorthodox tableau of Soviet people and historical events similar to *Ivan Lapshin* (see Chapter Two).

Gherman insists his revisionist treatments were not intentional provocations. His films were marginally released or shelved. None were allowed in festivals. Almost by chance *Twenty Days without War* was shown at Cannes in 1977, winning the Georges Sadoul Prize. *Ivan Lapshin* was quickly shelved and denied foreign distribution. *Trial on the Road* spent 15 years in captivity, for which the studio has now been fined.

Lana Gogoberidze

Tbilisi, 1500 Years (1959) (doc. w/ Tarkhan-Mouravi)
Under One Sky (1961)
I See the Sun (1965)
Frontiers (1970)
When Almonds Blossomed (1973)
The Little Incident/ Alarm (1975)
Several Interviews on Personal Questions (1979)
The Day Is Longer Than the Night (1984)
Full Circle/ Whirlpool (1987)

Lana Gogoberidze specializes in women's films. She and Kira Muratova were the first Soviet filmmakers to focus on female issues since Olga Preobrazhenskaya's groundbreaking 1927 movie, *Women of Ryazan.*

Gogoberidze's first feature, *Under One Sky*, is based on a collection of novellas about women from various periods of Georgian history. The next, *I See the Sun*, about a Georgian village in WWII, defines her unique publicistic style.

Her approach is best illustrated in *Several Interviews*, which is a polyphonic film about a female journalist (Sofiko) interviewing people of all ages whose lives, like her own, are falling apart. Gogoberidze deals with familiar themes: love, hope or lack of it, and loneliness, at the end of which she sees a bright future. Her film is a confession.

Gogoberidze lost her own father to the Stalin Terror and was brought up in children's homes and by an aunt. Her childhood fate (like the heroine of *Several Interviews*) is intertwined with the history of an estimated 30 million Soviet children without parents who faced similar circumstances. Gogoberidze repeats one flashback scene—a child's white figure jumping out of bed, surrounded by pitch blackness as she hears the soldiers' boots coming up the stairs—three times. The flashback is triggered in the journalist's memory by some facet of her interviews, such as people describing a favorite aunt, or an adulterous affair. It is at one point paralleled by the sound of her adulterous husband's footsteps coming home. The child's terror is echoed in the woman's fear about her wayward husband, but she now knows she shouldn't be afraid. She has found confidence; it is her personal triumph.

In a symbolic ending she strides along a street, smiling, thinking of her children who are free of fear. The Terror is behind them. The past won't haunt them any more. Its optimistic socialist-realist ending may have been a ploy to appease the censor. Nevertheless, Gogoberidze's film is a powerful exposé. It shows that Stalin was no kinder to his native Georgians than to other peoples of the USSR. Most Western film critics have never understood this movie properly because it is so rooted in local Georgian history.

Gogoberidze won the award for best director at the 1987 Tokyo Film Festival for *Full Circle*, another women's film. Two old friends, both middle-aged women, meet on a crowded sidewalk, have a conversation about past lovers, then part. One woman's loss is another's beginning.

Among other projects Gogoberidze has been directing a Soviet-British film, *A Waltz on the Pechora*, based on her mother's recollections of her exile north of the Arctic Circle.

Nikolai Gubenko/Goubenko

Nastasia and Fomka (1970) (his graduation film)
A Soldier Came Back from the Front (1972)
    (Shukshin's script)
If You Want to Be Happy (1974)
The Orphans/ War Waifs/
Wounded Game (1977)
From the Life of Holiday-Makers (1980)
Life, Tears and Love (1984)
Forbidden Zone/ Closed Zone (1987)

Gubenko, a fine screenwriter and director, and, under Gorbachev, the Minister of Culture, was the chief director of Moscow's Taganka Theater from 1987 to 1989. He is also a prolific actor and has starred in several of his own films. The films are mosaics of character portraits held together by his individualistic perspective which is always close to the people.

With the exception of *A Soldier Came Back*, a semi-documentary film about a post-war village, and *From the Life*, which is a satirical, vaudevillian comedy, all of Gubenko's films are perfect blends of serious and funny episodes with poetic intonations.

The soundtrack to *The Orphans* (titled *Podranki,* a hunting term for "wounded game") is so rich in audial motifs that they, together with visual bird imagery, make the script and dialogue seem cinematically redundant. From tangos, to birds singing, to people humming and whistling, to radios playing, to the music of Corelli, Marcello, and especially Vivaldi's *Four Seasons,* the film's narrative structure is the soundtrack.

The theme of war waifs applies to all the Soviet people, who, like these wounded birds were forced to learn to fly again (see Chapter 2). Another theme is memory, shown in the careful restoration of the orphanage's frescoes. By helping each other overcome the past, as Alyosha the hero tries to help Auschwitz survivor Gandin and his brothers Sergei (a thief) and Denis (an *apparatchik*), the country could again live. The choice is existential as in Dostoevsky's novel *The Brothers Karamazov,* which the director visually quotes in Alyosha-the-writer's adult scenes.

Although the concept of *Four Seasons* is reversed in Gubenko's view (an adult Spring and childhood Fall), one must pass from season to season, not dwelling in an eternal melancholy Winter. Gubenko and his wife, Janna Bolotova (object of Alyosha's infatuation), both play teachers/lovers in this unforgettable bitter-sweet movie.

Bolotova also stars in *Forbidden Zone,* Gubenko's first glasnost film. Shortly after a tornado swept the village of Volga-Vyatka, Gubenko visited the region with his camera and was struck by the change a storm lasting only a few minutes made in people's characters and relations. They had to decide what to restore and how to do it. Moreover, the storm had a cleansing effect, at least on some people, he said, and this is the central theme.

The soundtrack is an eerie, grating noise accompanying scenes of destruction, that turns out to be a cement-mixer (a leitmotif to destitute people's lives and a metaphor for government indifference). The poor villagers are left without shelter. Ironically, only the dachas of the rich vacationers survive. How far should their owners' compassion extend to victims of the closed zone? The area is sealed off from the press and public (proof of further alienation from the villagers), and the controlled news media issues a bitterly ironic official report of the *relief effort* (in fact, officials sell emergency supplies on the black market).

The film resembles the Maxim Gorky play *Vacationers* but unlike Gorky's irate peasants, Gubenko's villagers are passive in confrontations with the holidayers and officials, and the director chooses an epigraph from Chekhov: "Do Good!" Two types of Soviet intelligentsia are shown-the caring few like volunteer relief worker Vera Tretyakova (played by Bolotova) and the majority, who, without any conscience gobble up relief supplies.

The villagers include an invalid whose wife pleads for help and doesn't get it, and a widow who has scraped for 20 years to build her house, but is persuaded forcefully to move to town rather than having it restored. Pain, grief, uncertainty and horror are in her eyes as she is exiled and watches her home destroyed. Gubenko portrays the whole complexity of life and human nature brilliantly in this stinging allegory of the Soviet State and the isolation of its people.

Yuri Kara

Tomorrow There Came War (1987)
Kings of Crime (1988)

Kara got his start as a young director at the Gorky Studio for Children's and Youth Films. *Tomorrow,* his first movie, garnered prizes at numerous international festivals including The Special Jury Prize at the Youth Film Festival in Mannheim (West Germany), The Grand Prix "Golden Corn" in Valladolid (Spain) and "Big Amber—87" at the International Film Festival in Koshalin (Poland). His second film, *Kings of Crime,* a glasnost centerpiece, is an exposé of Soviet organized crime and won the USSR's distinguished Dovzhenko Golden Medal.

I watched *Tomorrow*'s debut with Alexander Chervinsky, the scriptwriter of Panfilov's *Theme.*

"It made me shudder," he said.

Chervinsky claimed he shared its vivid high school memories that recall Plumbum's world of black and white. Kara told us that he had trouble shooting it and getting it released. To be sure, Kara's portrayal of Komsomol camaraderie, friendship and love mixed with betrayal and nighttime arrests is stark and conventional, but no more so than the bleak, conservative epoch he describes.

The film is dedicated to Sergei Gerasimov (director, *Quiet Flows the Don* and VGIK teacher) and is based on a story by B. Vasiliev, who was apparently "an enemy of the people." The year is 1940. Iskra, the school's Komsomol leader (aptly named after Lenin's newspaper), lives with her severe Commissar mother, who used to love Lyuberetsky, the father of her classmate Vika. The father, a writer, is a friend of Mayakovsky, the famous revolutionary poet.

Vika, the romantic, reads Yesenin's love poetry (banned literature labelled Yeseninshchina—a hooliganistic/suicidal cult) and introduces Iskra and her friends to it at a reading in their opulent apartment. Someone informs on them. Her liberal father is arrested in the

THE VICTIM OF AN INFORMER: Lyuberetsky, the father of the romantic, idealistic heroine, Vika, in Yuri Kara's *Tomorrow There Came War* turns to look back at his daughter as he is arrested by the NKVD. Vika later commits suicide rather than give testimony against her father. (Photo: Courtesy Sovexportfilm)

night. Terror engulfs the school and Vika commits suicide in order not to testify against her father. Iskra also defies her teacher and her mother.

"There are no individuals, only citizens, and justice is what it appears to be to society," her mother says. She gives a heartfelt speech at Vika's funeral to the few terrified school friends who are brave enough to attend it.

What they don't know is that next year, in 1941, they will defend their country. The film ends with photos of Iskra and her mother, who were hanged as partisans, and of the friends and teachers who survived.

"It showed the real Stalinist period," Chervinsky said. "But in a new way—through a poetical young girl's eyes."

Elem Klimov

The Groom (1960)
Welcome, But/Or No Unauthorized Admission (1964)
Adventures of a Dentist (1965)
Sport, Sport, Sport (1971)
Agony/ Agonia/ Rasputin (1975), (Soviet Film Encyclopedia
  Kino, [Moscow. 1987], lists it as 1981). FIPRESSI
  Prize/Venice 1982, released in 1984)
And Still I Believe (Mikhail Romm's posthumous film
  completed with Marlen Khutsiev in 1976)
Larisa (1980) (doc. in memory of his late wife, Larisa
  Shepitko)
Farewell (Shepitko's posthumous film, started in 1979,
  finished by Klimov in 1981, first released in 1983)
Come and See (1985)

Klimov, chief architect of Soviet Cinema's glasnost revolution, was elected First Secretary of SFU in May, 1986. His stand-in at SFU, while he was on sabbatical making films, was Andrei Smirnov, a former colleague of Shepitko.

Welcome, his first real breakthrough into the movies, is a comedy—a satire on bureaucracy, that shows a Young Pioneers' summer camp run by an authoritarian director. In this hilarious parody of POW films, the hero Kostia tries to escape the camp, but when he fails he is hidden by his fellow "inmates" who spread a rumor of an "epidemic," the horror of which is paralleled by the chaos of parents' visting day.

The grotesque humor is fast-paced and the film looks like a propaganda poster aimed at Party politics and regimentation in Soviet society. Initially, Khrushchev banned it. One thing that caused the film to be questioned was the physical similarity between Kostia's grandmother and Khrushchev, as Kostia pictures her at her own funeral. The director was accused of wishing Khrushchev dead, until the premier saw the film, had a good laugh and ordered that it be released.

His second feature, *Adventures of a Dentist*, is based on a play by Alexander Volodin. Volodin, who had his own problems with the authorities, once sent the Minister of Culture his pen with a note: "Want to write my plays yourself?"

Volodin presented a script for *Adventures* to Romm who handed it to Klimov. It, too, is a satire. Characteristic of Klimov's early grotesque style, it takes aim at the suppression of talent and the individual. A young dentist (a Soviet Painless Parker) extracts teeth beautifully, but raises the ire of his unpopular colleagues. He is then forced to teach dentistry, but transmits his "secret" to a gifted student. Volodin's allegory on the artist's plight is echoed in Klimov's own difficulties with the censor. For instance, the *Agony/Rasputin* script got 169 "suggestions for improvement" on its first reading and was re-read six times by 30 people, then shelved. Ironically, it was meant to be a commemoration of the Bolshevik Revolution's 60th anniversary. In the film the mad monk Grigori Rasputin is portrayed with sympathy but revulsion and Czar Nicholas II is presented as weak-willed but good. It is a loosely jointed series of tableaux interspersed with black and white newsreel footage, old stills and historical commentary by a narrator. Klimov handles the transitions from black and white to color and back again with consummate skill. At times, transitions to black and white are used to emphasize the historical reality; group portraits being taken in color deftly dissolve to black and white stills, frozen in monochrome time to the crack of the photographer's magnesium flash. The sound simulates pistol shots. At other times, startling contrasts appear as black and white frames cut to color serving to underscore the unreality of the sumptuous decadence of the last days of the Russian court.

The Imperial Family, Rasputin and his hangers-on, and a noblewoman who sacrifices herself to the monk to save her husband from prison all appear in this aristocratic Who's Who of Petrograd/1916.[5] The Who who are missing on Klimov's list is even more intriguing: no Lenin or the proletariat, not to mention the Bolsheviks. Rasputin is portrayed as the essence of the peasantry. Rasputin, in the words of the Czarina, "*is* the people" and by implication the clay from which the Revolution was formed.

In addition to this docudrama, Klimov's documentaries include a memorial montage for his beloved wife, *Larisa*, and the bizarre collage

Sport, Sport, Sport (a genre-parody using dramatic episodes, sports contests, interviews, old films, pantomime and ballet).

Come and See is a title taken from *The Revelations of St. John* (Klimov loves to cite). Through the child's eyes of the hero Flor we see Nazi atrocity on an epic scale as Hitler's troops burn a Byelorussian village and all of its inhabitants alive (more than 600 settlements in Byelorussia were burned this way).

Like *Agony* and *Farewell, Come and See* is more than a realistic film. It is a patriotic, holy shrine. The film drew top prize at the Moscow Film Festival in 1985. (Re: *Farewell.* See Chapter 1.)

Andrei Konchalovsky/ Mikhalkov-Konchalovsky

A Boy and a Dove (1962) (w/ Evgeni Ostashchenko)
First Teacher (1965)
Asya's Happiness (1966)
A Nest of Gentlefolk (1969)
Uncle Vanya (1971)
Romance for Lovers (1974)
Siberiade (1979)

Since leaving the U.S.S.R. a decade ago under an official cloud, Konchalovsky has directed such Hollywood films as *Maria's Lovers, Duet for One, Shy People* and *Runaway Train.*

In 1987 at the Moscow International Film Festival, his brother, director Nikita Mikhalkov, who still lives and works in the U.S.S.R., was addressing a press conference when after some fidgeting, the outspoken Polish journalist/critic Piotr Cegielski stood up and asked Nikita the question that was on everybody's mind: "When will your brother visit the U.S.S.R.? When will you see him?"

Nikita pointed at the crowd.

"He's sitting in the seat right behind you," he said.

It was a symbolic reunion. Among the most insightful things Konchalovsky had to say were some comparisons he made between American and Soviet styles of filmmaking and their viewers.

"The American viewer expects a faster pace, minimal character and plot development," he said. "They are used to MTV and rock videos."

Of all the films he made, his favorite is *Asya's Happiness*, which is conspicuous by its absence from the new Soviet Film Encyclopedia.[6] It is an emotional and problematic movie about an ordinary teenaged girl growing up in a *kolkhoz*, criticized for its gloominess in depicting Soviet village life. It had a very limited release in 1966, but has finally been set free by the Conflict Committee. He does not think he could ever make another film like *Asya's Happiness*, after having adapted to Western filmic conventions, Konchalovsky told me, but to see this film again was for him personally the highlight of his visit and proof of perestroika. At last, in 1988, a Moscow retrospective of all his films was held and he received a general Soviet distribution.

His lifelong ambition has been to make a film about the Russian composer, Sergei Rachmaninov. He would consider making it as a U.S.S.R./U.S.A. co-production, he said, and has been collaborating on the screenplay with Yuri Nagibin, scriptwriter for Kurosawa's *Dersu Uzala*. Two other pictures then in the making were *Cinema Operator*, about a Russian family from 1938 to Stalin's death in 1953, and a rock opera version of Dostoevsky's *Crime and Punishment*.

Vyacheslav Kristofovich

A Lonely Woman Looking for a Companion (1987)

This superbly-acted comic jewel is about a likable alcoholic who answers a personal advertisement pinned to a telephone pole. In the light of Gorbachev's recent reforms it is a timely piece which realistically addresses daily concerns of Soviet society—alcoholism, urban alienation, divorce and women's issues.

Irina Kupchenko, who is noted for her understated style and brilliant dramatic roles in many of Mikhalkov's and Konchalovsky's films, received the best actress award in Montreal for her part in this picture. She has acted in numerous stage plays and TV films, and is also in Eldar Ryazanov's *Forgotten Melody for a Lonely Flute* (1987), the first comedy of perestroika.

Kupchenko plays the perfect foil to the sympathetic drunkard Valentin, acted by Alexander Zbruev, whose style is completely different from her own. This makes the odd couple believable as wills collide and their relationship twists and turns in imaginative, amusing, perhaps tragic ways. Klavdia, the lonely woman, is in her 40s, a dressmaker, brusque and straightforward, a stickler for cleanliness and order, who merely wants a man as an appendage to her comfortable life.

Valentin, the lonely man, is a disabled and divorced former circus performer who merely wants honest communication and has a sincere desire to reach out to others. The social evil, loneliness, stems from a callous lack of sympathy today, he reasons.

Klavdia's successful friend who "loves rich, useful people" gives unsolicited advice. Her boss gives only reprimands and insults Valentin. Her neighbor has affairs with married men. Young Pioneers who notice

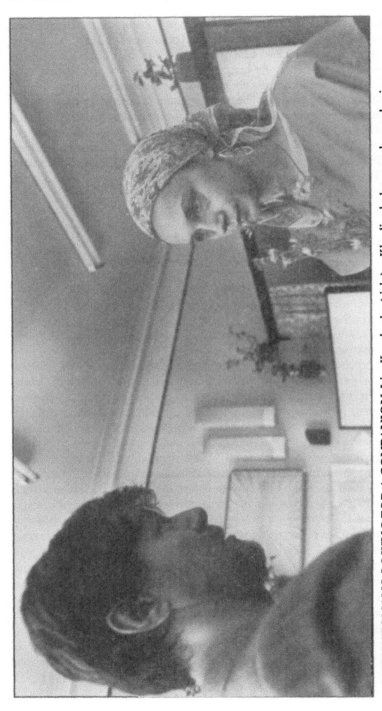

LONELY WOMAN LOOKING FOR A COMPANION: Irina Kupchenko (right) as Klavdia, the brusque dressmaker in Kristofovich's 1987 movie *Lonely Woman Looking for a Companion*, plays the perfect foil to Alexander Zbruev, as the sympathetic drunkard Valentin. (Photo: Courtesy Sovexportfilm)

her advertisement assume she is a hardship case and come to sing in her apartment.

There is no neat conclusion to this human story, but it is confidently told and strikes a familiar chord. Neither director Kristofovich, nor Kupchenko, with whom I spent considerable time in Moscow, felt that *A Lonely Woman* was a special movie. Shortly afterwards, however, the film received unanimous acclaim abroad and they were bombarded with questions ranging from curiosity about the hidden camera used to film long queues in front of wine shops to the effect of glasnost policy on the individual in his/her workplace.

Irakli Kvirikadze

The Pitcher (TV) *(1970)*
Down the Paths of Success (1971) (doc. TV)
The Celebrated (1973) (TV)
A Town Called Anara (1977)
The Swimmer (1982)
The Return of Almez (1985) (TV)

When he first showed The Swimmer, it was "like dropping a bomb in Goskino," according to Georgian director Irakli Kvirikadze. "That was 1982, Brezhnev's time, the most conservative era, and here I was showing the worst possible anti-Stalinist picture. The reaction was such that the acting director of Goskino, Pavlenok, had only one phrase for the movie: Burn it—both the print and the negative." [7]

The Swimmer wasn't burned, but it was severely edited to remove its anti-Stalinist message. For five years, only the censored version was officially sanctioned.

"I kept the uncut copy in my refrigerator," Kvirikadze told me. "And I took my copy around and showed it at various cinema clubs, but this brought me a lot of trouble, I was called before the authorities and was told to desist, that I had no right to show it, that I was breaking the law, but for me it was a matter of honor to show my film exactly as I had made it." [8]

In a small private screening room at the Mosfilm Studios in 1987, a dozen Western journalists, critics, and film distributors gathered to view for the first time inside the Soviet Union an officially authorized uncensored print of *The Swimmer.* The private screening was the result of an accident. A few days before at the film market for the 15th International Film Festival, the censored version of the film had been shown. In the storeroom someone had got the wrong print.

It wasn't the first such accident for Kvirikadze. Earlier that year at

THE SWIMMER: Irakli Kvirikadze's 1982 film was severely edited by Goskino censors during the Brezhnev era. The uncut version was unavailable until 1987. (Photo: Courtesy Sovexportfilm)

the San Remo Festival of Auteur Films in Italy, the restored original of *The Swimmer* had won the Grand Prix.

"When later I went to the Festival of Georgian Films at La Rochelle, France, imagine my horror when I discovered they were showing the censored version. It's a big problem," Kvirikadze said. "In the movie theater across the street, they have shown my film twice. I went to both performances and both played the cut version. After today's screening I'm going over there to retrieve the inferior copy, since my film is now allowed. But how can I run all over the world retrieving the other copies?"[9]

The censored version of *The Swimmer* holds together remarkably well as an artistic film, but without the cut scenes, an entire dimension of this multilayered picture is lost. The film is a three-generational retrospective told from the point of view of the grandson of a nonfictional hero of pre-revolutionary Georgia, Durmishkhan Dumbadze, a simple buffalo herder, who, responding to a dare, makes a marathon swim from Batumi to Poti, a distance of 60 kms. The famous English swimmer, Thomas Winston, fresh from a truimph at the La Manche marathon, is in Batumi with his elegant wife, the silent film star, Francesca Cottier. Durmishkhan boasts that he can swim twice as far.

"I'll jump in from the wharf and come out of the water in Poti. That's exactly twice the distance of La Manche," Durmishkhan claims. Three days later, dressed only in a loincloth, he emerges from the water in Poti. He catches a ride on a cart driven by a local monk, and returns to Batumi, where he announces his accomplishment to officials only to be accused of lying.

"I give you my word. I am a man," Durmishkhan protests, but he cannot prove his feat. He becomes a laughingstock, leaves town and descends into drunkenness. Then the revolution comes. In a particularly powerful scene in the uncensored version, the inebriated Durmishkhan is run over by a train in a railway tunnel. The audience sees the blackened interior and a subtitle announces: "The Coming of Soviet Power." Here the second part of the film begins, and its focus is Durmishkhan's son, Domenti. Like his father, he is a swimmer.

Domenti challenges a Stalinist hero, Odysseus Mesli, and qualifies for a marathon swim from Batumi to Poti, but Odysseus secretly denounces him, and before the swim is made, Domenti is arrested. He dies in a prison camp. Odysseus retains his title as Soviet champion and as an added bonus marries the beautiful Lala, who had been Domenti's wife. The uncensored print contains absurdly humorous scenes of the mass swimming events that were popular during Stalin's era—hundreds of people caught up in the Cult of the Body push garlanded rafts with huge portraits of the dictator about the harbor.

The third part of the film has a contemporary setting. Indeed *The Swimmer* in its unexpurgated edition can be seen as a Soviet social history—the descent of Soviet manhood—held together by the device of the swimming event. The grandson does not swim. He is very overweight and in no way resembles his father or his grandfather. He has neither physical nor spiritual strength.

"Why don't you swim?" a woman asks him.

He works for the group excursion bureau, he explains. He teaches tourists to sing Georgian songs. As the film ends, the grandson huddles in his luxury limousine to stay out of the rain, and looks out over the ocean.

Kvirikadze has made only a handful of feature length films. His works are often prize-winners, but they have rarely received adequate distribution and have often been blocked by censors. Much of his work is unknown in the Soviet Union because it was deemed unsuitable for Soviet audiences.

His 1977 comedy, *The Town Called Anara*, won several grand prizes at festivals of comedic film including the Silver Leopard at Locarno, but authorities at home suppressed it. The movie is based on a time-honored Georgian custom of drinking wine from large horns. The man who consumes the greatest volume of wine at a session takes possession of the largest horn as his prize. Prize horns usually hold about five liters. Drink this, remain standing, and the prize may be yours. But be prepared to defend your horn against all comers. According to custom, guests may come to your house and challenge you.

In the comedy *The Town Called Anara* the practice is made to appear grotesque. The prize horn holds seven liters. The father of the film's hero had originally won it, and his son, a tiny, shy man, must, as a matter of family honor, entertain all challengers. He sacrifices his work, his family and his love life for the sake of the tradition, and the absurd horn hangs over his head like the sword of Damocles. He is a slave to tradition and the tradition destroys him.

"It is as if *The Town Called Anara* had never appeared in the U.S.S.R., whereas Western audiences couldn't get enough of it," Kvirikadze told me. "At any screening I went to, people were just killing themselves laughing at it. Most of the Soviet theaters showed it for one night only. The same objections were always raised: it was too absurdist, and it showed Soviet reality to be a sea of alcoholism."

The director's 1985, made-for-TV production, *The Return of Almez*, received only one premier performance, which was scheduled at the same time as the U.S.S.R.'s prime time *Where, What, When* show.

"They bought the film and then they shelved it," said the director.

"Where, What, When is more popular than football. It was a kind of hari kari."

More recently, Kvirikadze teamed up with Nikita Mikhalkov to write a script for a film on the life of Alexander Griboyedov, the 19th century Russian playwright and ambassador to Tehran who was killed when a fanatical Persian mob stormed the embassy. The script, some 700 pages in length, is probably the longest in the history of Soviet film.

"The work could rival Bondarachuk's *War and Peace*—that's how ambitious it is," said Kvirikadze. Despite the massive endeavor, the film has never been made. "It would be just too expensive," the director said.[10]

Leida Laius

From Evening till Morning (1963)
The Milkman from Myaekula (1963)
The Forest Legend (1969)
A Spring in the Forest (1974)
A Man Is Born (1975) (doc.)
Childhood (1975) (doc.)
Tracks in the Snow (1975) (doc.)
The Keeper of Kyrboi (1980)
Games for Teenagers/Well, Come On, Smile (1986)
Stolen Date (1988)

Leida Laius' work, especially her searching docudrama *Games For Teenagers /Well, Come on, Smile,* is discussed at some length in Chapter 2.

Laius graduated from the Tallin Theatrical Institute in 1950 and VGIK in 1962. She acted with the Kingiseppe Theater Company and has been working at the Tallin Film Studio (now Tallinfilm) since 1960. In 1979 she was recognized as a State Artist of the Estonian S.S.R.

Laius' early works are screen adaptations of Estonian literary classics: *From Evening till Morning* (based on M. Kaidu's story), *The Milkman from Myaekula* (E.Vilde's work), *The Forest Legend* (from A. Kitsberg's play *The Werewolf*), *A Spring in the Forest* (based on V. Saar's novel *Ukuaru*), and *The Keeper of Kyrboi* (from A. Tammseare's story). Before her original feature film *Games for Teenagers*, she had also made several documentary films, including *A Man Is Born, Childhood,* and *Tracks in the Snow.*

Her 1988 production, *Stolen Date*, is about a woman who abandons her child.

Konstantin Lopushansky

Solo (1983)
Letters from a Dead Man(1986)
Expulsion from Hell (1988)
Visitor to a Museum (1989)

Lopushansky was Tarkovsky's assistant director for Stalker and shares with the prolific and much-banned Lenfilm director, Alexander Sokurov, the distinction of being Tarkovsky's rightful heir, although it is Sokurov who wears the mantle. Both represent the Leningrad school of filmmaking and are the leaders of the spiritual avant-garde in Soviet cinema.

Solo, his short diploma film, is a powerful, surreal movie about a musician performing in Shostakovich's 7th Symphony which is being broadcast to Britain from WWII-besieged Leningrad. Bombed trams and houses suggest a Tarkovskian landscape similar to the master's *Stalker* though not relieved by its obligatory *pastorale*.

Tarkovsky's disturbing, heavily textured sensibility is repeated in Lopushansky's debut color feature *Letters from a Dead Man*, which won a record of 14 international prizes. Like *Solo* it shows a postwar catastrophic environment seen from a culture that has experienced war firsthand. It stands in perfect contrast to the ABC-TV production *Amerika* and parallels *The Day After*. *Letters* is a sobering parable from the glasnost side of what used to be the Iron Curtain. It played on Ted Turner's cable network in the U.S.A. in 1987.

With the caveat that war is waged not for policy interests but *accidentally* (hot coffee in the button-pusher's mouth!), Lopushansky's film is terrifying and believable. Novice science fiction writer Vyacheslav Rybakov, seasoned *Stalker* veteran Boris Strugatsky and Lopushansky combined on the writing of the screenplay, with Lenfilm's Gherman suggesting the *fantastic letters* genre as the formal montage device.

The post-bomb tradition in Western cinema is traceable to the late '50s and Stanley Kramer's *On the Beach*, about which Romm remarked: "Nothing seems amiss, only a strange sound—a horse's hoofs [no more gasoline] and the audience's reaction to this film about the world's end is laughter [as] there is not a single corpse!" [11]

Lopushansky tackles the post-bomb fantasy with harsh realism. In his film there are no horses, no laughter, and corpses are everywhere. In

LETTERS FROM A DEAD MAN: In Lopushansky's post-holocaust rationalist state sick or parentless children are excluded from the Central Bunker and left to fend for themselves. (Photo: Courtesy Sovexportfilm)

the process he shows the human tragedy closer to the abyss than Kramer did, and he makes a real innovation—he shows a moral restoration of the world in the midst of post-apocalyptic tragedy.

Post-nuclear-holocaust films are a difficult genre for the artist. The propagandistic aspect of the anti-war topic, if shown in all its visual horror, may easily overwhelm the artistic elements of the theme. Tarkovsky and Kramer, for example, capture the spirit of impending moral danger without explicit scenes of devastation; Lopushansky does both.

Lopushansky's surviving state is neo-Fascist. His political thesis is clear, as doctors in the film select which children will be permitted in the Central Bunker. Many of the children are afflicted with muteness after the blast, and are deemed unfit, shunned, and left to die. Even if the child is healthy, but without parents, he or she will be excluded. The human antithesis to the new rationalist state is found in Larsen, the Nobel-prize-winning atomic scientist who agonizes over his profession and composes rhetorical letters to his dead son Eric.

His communion with the "mute" orphans is the film's prophetic spiritual synthesis. Larsen, played by Rolan Bykov, in protective suit and gas-mask leaves his colleagues in their museum basement and steps into the upper world where he finds the outcast children and a Protestant pastor sheltered in a church. Together they celebrate Christmas after the apocalypse. A Biblical voiceover (superdubbed over an invisible child's Latin prayer) intones from the New Testament of Being: "The world did not perish! Thus he [Larsen] taught them. And led them to gaze at the first evening star. And spake: Behold! There was no star. The world was darkness."

The symbolism is subtly preserved in sepia hues and bluish tints. In a long flashback scene, rockets blast off and the scientist's head is bathed in light and water for penance. In another scene, a girl washes his waxen face, an ablution in preparation for burial. The final shot is unforgettable: masked children trudging up a radioactive hill to seek the promised Star of Bethlehem!

The director's prayer for humanity is echoed in another way in *Expulsion*. Another fantasy-flick, it is prompted by his concern for ecological restraint. Scientists say that Nature resists the human ecological "onslaught" with an antidote that causes genetic change. An atmospheric catastrophe wreaks genetic havoc, which only a handful of people dare hope to escape.

Lopushansky well deserves his prize for Best Director of Fantasy Films (Madrid) and the support of Gorbachev if Soviets, like Westerners, love our planet.

Nikita Mikhalkov

A Quiet Day at War's End (1971)
Friend Among Strangers/ Stranger Among Friends (1974)
Slave of Love (1976)
An Unfinished Piece for a Player Piano (1977)
Five Evenings (1979)
Oblomov (1980)
Kinfolk (1982)
Without Witnesses (1983)
Dark Eyes (1987)

In Mikhalkov, we will not find a starry-eyed revolutionary, who is willing to turn upside down the entire film industry, purging the last remnants of old for the new. His taste in film themes tends to the safe and conservative. He is, in the true spirit of *democratizatsia,* a liberal, who, while he personally supports the essence of the changes now in progress, courageously came to the defense of socialist-realist colleague Sergei Bondarachuk when radical members of the SFU condemned the traditionalist as a reactionary and sought his explusion from the union. Bondarachuk, though he is politically archconservative, is noted for such masterworks as his definitive Oscar-winning eight-hour film version of Tolstoy's *War and Peace.*

"We cannot deny that Bondarachuk is an artist," Mikhalkov told the Secretariat.

Mikhalkov, who already has links to the West through his emigre brother Andrei Konchalovsky, was one of the first Soviet filmmakers to take advantage of the increased opportunities for participation in foreign productions that have come about from perestroika. His 1987 Italian picture *Dark Eyes* stars Marcello Mastroianni in a role based on Chekhov's story *The Lady and the Lap Dog* and three other short works— *My Wife, The Birthday Party,* and *Anna on the Neck.*

"Marcello is a Chekhovian-type actor who knows the art of semitone and understatement, and who is capable of conveying three pages of a book in just one glance," says Mikhalkov. "The purpose was not to translate Chekhov stories to the screen," according to the director, "but to create a Chekhovian environment, respecting the spirit rather than the letter of his work." [12]

The result is a film which is the meeting of two great cultures, as Mastroianni plays the part of the great Italian lover Romano opposite one of the U.S.S.R.'s most celebrated young actresses, Elena Safonova, with support from an illustrious international cast.

Elena Safonova is Anna, the unattainable Russian heroine who is the object of Romano's fervent love. She is married to Manlio (Paulo Baroni). Romano is also married, and has a mistress. His wife Elisa (Silvana Mangano) is a wealthy heiress, while Romano, though he is charming, has a modest background. He is waited on hand and foot; he becomes a buffoon and a lap dog.

"Everything became automatic, even love," he says reflecting on his marriage. Then Elisa brings him the terrible news: the family is on the verge of bankruptcy. Confronted with problems, Romano takes the easy route and runs away to a spa. There he is kept busy by women who seek brief affairs, and he justifies his presence by claiming that his legs feel "fragile."

Flirting with Anna, he says he will get better if only she will whisper a Russian word in his ear. She says *sabatchka,* which means "lap dog," and he pretends immediately to revive. Later he charms her by walking into a mudpool in his all-white suit to retrieve her hat which the wind has blown off. They make love. He is touched by her modesty and unexplained tears. She too is smitten, but flees back to Russia, leaving behind a scented letter. She is married; she is ashamed the letter says; she loves him but she doesn't want to see him again. Romano falls madly in love and determines to go to Russia to find her.

In Anna's home town Romano sees a little white dog and hears heavenly music. He follows it and finds Anna. They embrace. She says she will leave her pompous husband, but first he must tell his wife everything. Divinely happy, he returns to Italy where he discovers that Elisa has found the scented letter.

"Tell me the truth," she demands. "Do you love a woman in Russia?" He hesitates and says no. Elisa tears up the note and with it her husband's future.

In a bitter-sweet ending, Romano has left Elisa after all. It is many years later. He works as a waiter on a cruise ship. Anna is a passenger on board, but she no longer recognizes him.

Mikhalkov is a perfectionist, and an exquisite craftsman. He takes command of every detail that the camera sees. His style suits perfectly the classic models that he uses with other films such as his re-creation of Ivan Goncharov's *Oblomov* and *An Unfinished Piece for Player Piano,* which like others of his films is based on Chekhov. The period piece is the director's forte. The exception is his contemporary psychological drama *Without Witnesses,* which brings to the screen an unstaged play by Sofia Prokofieva.

Without Witnesses is an important film because it addresses the theme of secret denunciations, although in purely cinematic terms it is undeniably his weakest production. The film is a psychodrama acted out by only two characters, a man and his ex-wife. Late at night the man arrives at his former spouse's apartment intent on reclaiming her by manipulation and intimidation. Her lover is his boss and the ex-husband has written a secret letter of denunciation against him. At the cinematic level, however, the film falls into the classic trap of being much too staged. Heavy-handed rhetorical devices, such as actors halting the action to present a monologue to the audience, undercut the motion picture's dynamics, and the melodramatic plot, which would be worthy of pre-Chekhovian theater, is too conservative to be good contemporary cinema.

Mikhalkov, like his older brother Andrei Mikhalkov-Konchalovsky, studied with Mikhail Romm at VGIK. His early films, *A Quiet Day at War's End* and *Stranger Among Friends,* brought him critical acclaim, but it was his 1976 work about the pre-revolutionary film industry, *Slave of Love,* which brought him to international prominence. *Slave of Love* is a multi-layered film, rich in the pyschological subtlety and filmic metaphor which is characteristic of the director, and at the same time it is marked by sharp contrasts in action which are touched by moments of humor and parody. It is at once a romantic love story, a tale of Bolshevik heroism in the conventional socialist-realist mold, and a statement about the nature of film itself. This depth is apparent from the first scene. The film opens as a comedic imitation of the early silent cinema complete with piano music, but cuts quickly to a shot of the audience where armed men disrupt the presentation to arrest one of the viewers. The illusion of the film medium and the reality of revolution are thus shown in immediate and dramatic contrast.

Mikhalkov comes from a celebrated artistic background. His great-grandfather and great-great-grandfather were painters. His father and his mother are both writers. He, himself, began his career as an actor at the Shchukin School of Theater in Moscow. As this book went to press, the director and screen writer Rustan Ibragimbekov were making a Soviet-U.S.-Italian co-production *The Barber of Siberia* , which would be another period piece showing Russia at the turn of the last century. The plot, according to Ibragimbekov, concerns a love affair between a young Russian officer and an American woman who comes to Russia where her father works.

Kira Muratova

By the Steep Ravine (w/ Alexander Muratov) *(1962)*
[Our] Honest Bread (w/ Alexander Muratov) *(1965)*
Brief Encounters (1967)
Long Farewells (1971)
Getting to Know the Big Wide World (1979)
Among Gray Stones (1983)
Change of Fortune/Destiny (1987)

The Asthenic Syndrome (1989)

When I first heard Ms. Muratova (in a capacity audience at the Vancouver Film Festival), she did not mince her words: "My country had reached bankruptcy and there was nowhere else for it to go. Everything had to burst!" [13]

Although her full career has not been documented, rumors abound about this enigmatic, unobtrusive woman who bears an uncanny physical resemblance to Fellini's wife (Gulietta Massina) in *Juliet of the Spirits,* and whose surface placidity baffled her superiors.

In an interview with *San Francisco Chronicle* film reporter Judy Stone, she said: "They thought I was a non-threatening woman until I started to shoot films. Then they asked themselves: What kind of a monster is she?" [14]

I spent the whole day at the Vancouver Festival talking with "the monster." At her insistence, we drank cokes, ate chocolates and smoked only *her* favorite Soviet cigarettes (lit with Kin-dza-dzian matches that kept spluttering and breaking). We spoke in Russian, English, and French (her third language after Rumanian) as she zestily celebrated her life. Contrary to popular gossip this woman is extremely humorous in her attitude toward life.

"People don't understand my humor," she said.

She is definitely misunderstood. As a result, her films, unlike Lana Gogoberidze's, have been severely maligned. Half her works are not listed in the 1987 Soviet Film Encyclopedia, *Kino.*

Muratova said because she is a painter who enjoys solitude, she has "a somewhat undeserved hermit's reputation." She feels unselfconscious about her works and does not bother to "explain" them: "They're only art!" Her films "just happen," are apolitical psychodramas and have been labelled "bourgeois," which, in a sense, they are.

Upon her films' release, official critics who had not seen them earlier were perplexed, as they could find nothing that was politically "sharp." Muratova is not a typical Soviet filmmaker due to her family background which is partly Western, making her an internal emigre in outlook. She was born in Rumania in Soroki/Soroka, which is now in the Moldavian S.S.R., and was brought up by a Russian grandmother while both her parents who were in the Communist "underground" were imprisoned. They had also lived in Belgium.

In 1954 Muratova moved to the U.S.S.R., went to MGU (Moscow State University) for a year, then dropped her studies to enter VGIK and to participate in Sergei Gerasimov's workshop. Later she joined the Odessa Film Studio. She made her first two films with Alexander Muratov, her ex-husband who is now a director at the Kiev Film Studio. The first, *By the Steep Ravine*, is their diploma film on a contemporary scenario. Their second, *Honest Bread*, describes a conflict between a kolkhoz chairman and an inept Party boss. Everyone connected with the movie was accused of looking gloomily at agricultural affairs.

Brief Encounters, scripted by leading feminist Natalya Ryazantseva, is Muratova's first women's film and a solo creation which catapulted her far ahead of her contemporaries of both sexes.

"My troubles were circumstantial," she says. "Glasnost is my offspring (*moi ptenets*), not vice versa."

Creature of glasnost that she is, her layered psychological films rise above the social pale, while still confronting the era of stagnation. She focuses on the private life and narrow, local matters.

Newly arrived in Odessa with her husband, Kira saw housing and water supply shortages and made her heroine Valentina in *Brief Encounters* an executive who deals with these problems. She played the role herself—her first and last appearance as an actress.

Maxim, Valentina's husband, is acted by the late dissident poet/balladeer/actor Vladimir Vysotsky (the U.S.S.R.'s "Bob Dylan").

"He was thrust upon me," she said. "*Ego mne vsunuli.*"

Vysotsky plays a merry, dare-devil geologist. A third character, Nadia (played by Nina Ruslanova in her first acting role), and her funny girlfriend Lyuba are unadorned country girls. Lyuba looks for city glitter, while Nadia waitresses in a tea-room until she finds Maxim and spends a few days with him and his wife. Maxim opens her eyes to life's joys and Valentina displays wisdom and generosity. Nadia, who had met and fallen in love with Maxim while he was on a rural geological mission, discovers through her "encounter" with the couple that their love is genuine and she leaves them and the small world of tea-rooms to go back to her village.

Encounters is an experimental black and white raw-stock movie. Only six prints were made and it was, in effect, banned. Like Kirghiz/Lenfilm director Dinara Asanova (d. 1985), she relies on improvisation and prefers to use non-professional actors. Vysotsky's performance is artful, but Muratova was disappointed with it.

"He almost ruined my picture with his romanticism," she said.[15]

Why was the film outlawed? Officials objected to her showing Odessa's shortages and her nonjudgmental portrayal of a potential love triangle. Tenants, for whom the housing administrator Valentina is responsible, carry well-water to their new but shoddy winter apartments since the plumbing is incomplete. A butcher trims off two

BRIEF ENCOUNTERS: Kira Muratova (right) performed opposite late dissident poet-balladeer Vladimir Vysotsky (left) in her 1967 production *Brief Encounters*. (Photo: Courtesy Sovexportfilm)

grams of sausage to make a profit for himself. Stockings run. Doorknobs come off brand new doors. Geologists make illicit money from their expeditions, and Nadia helps Valentina compose a letter to the Comrades, the topic sentence of which is: "Everything written about agriculture is bullshit!" All that Muratova portrays was a part of daily life in 1967 Odessa. The frankness with which she recorded the backdrop was, nevertheless, two decades ahead of its time. "It is preposterous to imagine me a social critic," she maintains. The careful viewer would agree.

Grand corruption, even *Guess Who's Coming to Dinner* style satire, is not Muratova's approach. The eye follows bustling camera work. Scenically linked images are supported by a choppy soundtrack, pans, and blurs. *Brief Encounters* swarms with ideas, with illogicality and paradox. It is a psychological microcosm, sometimes adorned with filigree, sometimes unadorned.

The characters are romantic men (such as Lyuba's gentle, pig-faced farmer-boyfriend who was rejected by the Army) and frustrated, alienated women who live like bachelors. All are strangely molded by their environment and have no resolution in relationships. All find sympathy on Muratova's canvas.

The roving camera and narrative structure is more disturbed in her second black and white feature *Long Farewells*, which was blacklisted for 16 years for aesthetic reasons and its bourgeois topic—an aging mother with an astonishing variety of wigs (one for each suitor) who feels she's losing her teenaged son. Alienated by their own intellectuality, they are barely sympathetic characters, though humorous and loving in rare heart-to-heart moments. Yevgeniia is a professional translator in Odessa and Sasha is a lonely boy who dreams of joining his teacher-father in Novorosiisk. The father sends him letters to a railway P.O. box and calls long-distance for three minutes while mother listens at the booth and sends a telegram: "Leave us alone!" Unlike Miroshnikov (*Messenger Boy*) he does not hurl assagais or make bonfires in the kitchen but fantasizes sarcastic poetry and watches slides of peacocks, butterflies and birds as mother nags and spends hours applying jars of makeup with a safety-pin at her figurine-lined vanity.

Long Farewells consists almost entirely of audio-visual details created through montage and collage, and conveys mother/son tensions through disjointed editing and repeated musical cacophony, or through Sasha's whistling *Yellow Submarine*. A Chekhovian mood is established with a shot of an injured seagull at the beginning and a climactic workers concert with mime where Yevgeniia creates a scandal.

Farewells ends as Sasha comforts her and she discards her wig and sings "A Lonely Sail." Muratova's still-life vignette has nothing to do with Soviet reality. In the screen's blinking eye we see Buñuel, Marnie, and Dali. Regrettably, her early films are not in color. *Farewells* opens with a brilliant cinematic image of a hand pulling hydroponic plants out of the water and holding up the roots. Only a Soviet Red Star shining in the background connects us to the setting.

"We're all like plants," says the naturalist/geologist in *Brief Encounters*. But the plant without the soil, with nothing to root it, is like one of Muratova's intellectual characters and like herself, who was twice uprooted in disrepute and left in internal exile.

Farewells marks the end of Muratova's black-and-white period and might have marked the end of her motion picture career as she was subsequently forced to quit filmmaking and to work for several years at a variety of other jobs. Her color period began with Lenfilm's offer to direct *The Big, Wide World* about the love lives of construction workers. In the film, a woman chooses between two men. It had no trouble passing censors, but it was not without impact on her career.

"Goskino said it showed gray, uncouth, stupid types and I was banned from filming contemporary subjects," Muratova told me.

The Big, Wide World is Muratova's favorite film, however, because it is "the most organic and nonjudgmental." Her lens turned thereafter to Vladimir Korolenko's 1880s story, *Underground Children*, a Russian *Les Miserables* which she titled *Among Gray Stones*. The picture caused an even greater furor. Her negative was cut, and she tried to delete her name from the credits.

With glasnost her destiny changed, thus *Change of Fortune* seemed an apt title for a film version of Somerset Maugham's story *The Letter*, in which she features the Russian emigré actress Natalia Leble (another glasnost first!) and deals with a favorite theme—passion. It is the tale of a young society woman, Maria, who murders her lover, claiming self-defense but conceals her true relationship from her husband and her lawyer. Maugham's vain, cynical characters are slaves to their passions, yet spiritually free and human, a paradox that suits Muratova's style as she probes their relationship and seeks an image to reflect the interaction of wealth, power and hypocrisy.

The *Asthenic Syndrome*, named for the medical condition which may render a person extremely weak or passive, is a montage of loosely related vignettes of contemporary Soviet society, and a strangely surreal vision of social decay.

Muratova has been intriguing film audiences around the world with her individualistic style, her uncompromising honesty and with the unusualness of her vision. Against apparently banal backdrops, her films delve deeply into loneliness and the problems of human communication.

Hence they strike a universal chord and are larger than politics or the culture that spawned them. Muratova is singular—unique!

Valeri Ogorodnikov

The Burglar (1987)

At the Festival of Leningrad Youth Films held in the spring of 1987, Ogorodnikov's first feature film, *The Burglar*, drew the attention of critics and distributors who for once agreed that here was a rock film that bridged the generation gap. Although it targeted young audiences, it reinforced values that hardly raised the ire of adults.

The problem of developing a film language that could address Soviet youth has become important to New Model filmmakers. For some of the older Soviet generation, rock culture is seen as Sergei Mikhalkov (director Nikita Mikhalkov's father) has labelled it—"the moral equivalent of AIDS." Others conveniently explain it away as youthful immaturity, a peripheral manifestation of the larger culture. However, to see rock music as a minor part of larger society denies its subterranean vitality.

Youthful Soviet followers cannot be blamed for idolizing contemporary rock stars. They are preoccupied with questions of which their fathers are unaware. The older generation may have vaguely heard of Kostia Kinchev, leader of the group Alisa who stars in *The Burglar*, Boris Grebenshchikov, whose music is featured in Soloviev's film *ASSA*, or the group Kino, but any comparison of rock culture with Soviet mass culture blurs generational values into a single rhythm and denies rock culture its identity.

Before glasnost, if cinema used rock music at all, it was only to create a negative background, but music is only one expression of the culture which grew out of rock and roll style; the culture itself was a grouping of youth around alternative values. For instance, Alexei Kozlov, Soviet composer and band leader of Arsenal, now in his 50s, was a member of the 1950s youth cult known as Stilyagi (from the Russian word *stil*, style), who proudly adopted the insulting nickname to denote stylish music and manners in contrast to the bleak conformity of Stalinist tastes. [16]

Current confessional Leningrad rock typified by Kinchev is ironic and sometimes aggressive, but most of all it is honest. His songs, like Grebenshchikov's, are open, in contrast to the spiritually, emotionally and intellectually stifling "recommended" pop product found in restaurants, official concerts, and hotels. Rock counterculture opposes this packaged musical consumerism which has imposed values of obedience

THE BURGLAR: As the first rock film of Lenfilm's spiritualist revivalist movement, *The Burglar* has attained the same reputation in the U.S.S.R. as Norman Jewison's *Jesus Christ Superstar* has in the West. (Photo: Courtesy Sovexportfilm)

and optimistic well being on the Soviet masses. The music that has emerged through glasnost from the underground may be naive and vulnerable, but its strength is its outspokenness.

Although there have been half a dozen rock features since 1970, starting with *Four White Shirts* about Latvian hippies and rockers, and there have been teenage comedies and melodramas spotlighting occasional stars and hit songs between 1981 and 1987, *The Burglar* is a landmark film in its unequivocal choice of subject matter (juvenile delinquents and rock musicians), and in its thematic approach. For Ogorodnikov, young people have become superheroes. As the first Soviet rock movie of Lenfilm's spiritual revivalist movement, it has earned the same reputation in the U.S.S.R. as Norman Jewison's *Jesus Christ Superstar* and Milos Forman's *Hair* did in the West. Although it is only a detective story, like these earlier rock musicals it heralds the dawning of an era, a new Age of Aquarius that preaches "love and understanding" for all.

The director adopts the cinematic viewpoint of Senia, a preadolescent schoolboy. Senia's mother is dead. His father is an alcoholic. The sensitive lad idolizes his older brother, the amateur rocker Kostia, played by Kinchev. After a quarrel with his father, Kostia vanishes into Leningrad's cellars, attics, and the Cafe Saigon where rock music enthusiasts hang out. Senia, who has been placed in a state boarding school, goes looking for him. Within the complex dynamic that unfolds, the objective camera roams the dens of Leningrad pop. Ogorodnikov emphasizes reason over emotion, but the camera nevertheless reveals an amoral, chaotic world. His unadorned look at the underground, however, is tempered by a world view that rises above the environment and by sentimental internal sequences such as those where Kostia communicates with his dead mother. In the Saigon Cafe amateur groups compete in a battle of the bands, while a bored older judge shuts his eyes, and in an adjacent scene the young people's naive efforts to assert themselves are mirrored in a TV screen showing Dostoevsky's *Poor Folk*. *Poor Folk* is one key to *The Burglar*. This is the novel that launched Dostoevsky's career, much as *The Burglar* is Ogorodnikov's debut opus. In the novel, the downtrodden characters Devushkin and Varenka find an unorthodox love and seek to carve out a spiritual identity in an alienated urban landscape. In *The Burglar* the young musicians through their harsh but ecstatic rock culture search for a way out of their own underground. Ogorodnikov's mist-shrouded Leningrad is Dostoevsky's St. Petersburg in modern guise. The inhabitants of cheap communal apartments cluster in groups for protection with few illusions, but somehow out of the squalor transcendent values emerge.

Kostia is almost broken by his environment but is blessed with a talent that none of the other musicians possess. When he sings to his comrades their faces light up in generational solidarity. He resists being crushed and hitches them to his own rising star.

> Yes, I burned my bridge.
> A toast to those who couldn't cross it!
> In these damp underground vaults
> There are others like me and like you.
> We don't step aside here
> And don't cover our eyes—
> Not for us compromise!

The film opens with the theme of the Sorcerer from Tchaikovsky's *Swan Lake*, which is played by Senia's school band. This musical epigraph parallels the conflict between Kostia, the poet, and his own evil sorcerer, the metalist and motorcycle gang leader Khokhmach. Khokhmach, whose name means buffoon, preys on groupies and hates the new music and its message. He tries to subvert Kostia's talent and to silence his philosophy. He also extorts payment for the synthesizer he has loaned Kostia, even though the instrument is now in someone else's hands. The dark-haired brute with bulging biceps demands Kostia steal it back.

"I am a singer, not a burglar," says Kostia. Senia overhears him and thinks he can save his brother by retrieving the instrument himself.

The biker subculture is portrayed as an ally of urban chaos blocking the way of the artist's righteous path. Kostia must fight the gang at the risk of his life. As Kostia's inner conflict develops, the ballet leitmotif is replaced by refrains from the Catholic mass and a visual mirage effect of spectres in the sky, pointing to Kostia's spiritual ascendency over the gang which surrounds him. For now he appears lost—a sinner with little hope. Wrecking the abandoned streetcar in which he lives, he cries out: "We can be martyred, but not betrayed."

Even though he is attuned to the chorus of his own generation, he is tragically deaf to the voice of his brother which professes "love!" He couldn't care less about his younger sibling until Senia is charged with stealing the synthesizer. The boy is a nuisance.

Senia's arrest leads to an uncomfortable and incomplete reunion between Kostia and his father. At the end of the film, Senia is shown with his back to a wall. The last chords of the mass sound.

Tolomush Okeyev

All About Horses (1965) (doc.)
The Sky of Our Childhood (1967) (his first feature)

Boom *(1968)* (doc.)
Mountain Necklace *(1969)* (doc)
Muras *(1969-70)* (doc.)
Hunting Birds *(1970)* (doc.)
The Heritage (1970)
Worship the Fire (1972) (semi–doc)
The Ferocious One (1974)
The Red Apple *(1975)* (based on a novella by
    Chingiz Aitmatov)
Ulan *(1977)* (semi–doc)
The Golden Autumn (1981)
The Descendant of the Snow Leopard (1985)
Mirages of Love *(1987)* (U.S.S.R.—Syrian co-production)

The semi-documentarist Tolomush Okeyev was born in a felt tent in the mountains of Kirghizia in 1935. His father was a herdsman and in the year of Tolomush's birth, Stalin was bringing forced collectivization to the nomadic peoples of this Central Asian republic. It was an era Okeyev was later to recreate in his feature *Worship the Fire* about Urkui Salieva, the republic's first woman communist, and her murder at the hands of religious reactionaries.

Worship the Fire, like all of Okeyev's films, seeks a balance between the inexorable forces of modernization and nostalgia for the traditional. Like Larisa Shepitko, in her posthumous *Farewell*, he is noted for an environmental focus.

The history of Soviet film and that of the modern Kirghizian state are interwoven. The Kirghizian language did not have an alphabet until 1922. In the '20s, Dziga Vertov's *Kino Pravda* and other newsreels helped to educate the then illiterate population of this remote region which borders on China to the south, Uzbekistan to the west, and the steppes of Kazakhstan to the north. At the same time early documentarists recorded the proud culture of the horsemen who lived close to nature and drank fermented mare's milk, *kumyss*.

The Kirghizfilm Studio was established in 1955. In the '60s it progressed from documentaries to features and engaged Andrei Konchalovsky to make his film debut, *The First Teacher*, based on Kirghizian writer Chingiz Aitmatov's story of the same name. *The First Teacher* was a kind of visual homage to the early documentarists, a collection of village vignettes, set in the '20s. Shepitko's 1963 Kirghizfilm production *Heat* is also based on an Aitmatov work, his novella *The Camel's Eye*. Okeyev was an assistant soundman for *Heat*, but four years later he was directing his own first feature, *The Sky of Our Childhood*, another '20s retrospective.

The psychological *Sky of Our Childhood* has earned a special place in the history of Soviet film as one of the seminal works of the Kirghizian school which includes Melis Ubykeyev (who is noteworthy for his *White Mountains* showing Kirghizia in the midst of the Civil War) and Bolotbek Shamshiyev (who performed in Shepitko's *Heat*, and whose *Echo of Love* is yet another adaptation of an Aitmatov piece—*On the River Baidamtal*).

In *The Sky of Our Childhood*, Kalyka, a city schoolboy, returns to his native village and to his herdsman father, Bakai. Road construction is beginning to change the ancient grazing grounds. Bakai is forced to move his horse herds to a new pasture and many other changes ensue. The changes, however, are shown without didacticism or social rhetoric. This non–judgmental objectivism did not enamor Okeyev to the officials of Goskino.

The film neither glorifies traditional values nor falsifies the benefits or harmfulness of modernization. Instead, it focuses on the effects of change upon the individual characters and delivers its message through unexplained visual metaphor. Bakai's sons want to move to town. Bakai refuses. The father has tamed a golden eagle, but is forced to set it free. The bird has forgotten how to fly. In the end, the once noble eagle is stuffed—placed by ignorant construction workers atop a stone idol venerated by the nomads.

All this is in keeping with the developing tradition of the Kirghizian cinema, which has attempted not so much to immortalize the course of events, as to assess the new events of the evolving world—to understand the contemporary epoch, its sensibilities and accomplishments, while recording the life of its people in all its complexity.

Okeyev's sense of truth has been regarded as cruel by some Soviet critics. For example, his Syrian co-production, *The Mirages of Love*, portrays the Oriental Renaissance in Khiva and Bukhara, but in an unexpected way. The film's protagonist, the artist Mani, is from his youth supremely gifted, but others are jealous and cut off his hand. Against an intricate tapestry of natural and artistic beauty, common mortals strike out against the divine and destroy it. Considering his portrayal of the ancient Tamerlane Empire, we may expect more of the unexpected in his anticipated epic *Genghis Khan*.

Like the Kirghizian writer Chingiz Aitmatov, Tolomush Okeyev is involved in politics. Aitmatov is a member of the Supreme Soviet of the U.S.S.R. and Okeyev is Deputy of the Supreme Soviet of the Kirghiz Republic. Unadorned openness seems to come naturally to these two. When Aitmatov rose to nominate Gorbachev as Soviet President in June 1989, he reminded the Congress of the nominee's mistakes—the flagging economy, and turbulence among ethnic groups. Okeyev, the environ-

MIRAGES OF LOVE: Okeyev's 1987 Syrian co-production portrays the Oriental Renaissance in Khiva and Bukhara against a backdrop of artistic and natural beauty. (Soviet Poster Art: Courtesy Sovexportfilm)

mentalist, has been active in Sovexportfilm's drive to encourage U.S.-U.S.S.R. co-productions.

At the Second Entertainment Summit of U.S. and Soviet Filmmakers in 1988 in Moscow he gave the toast to end the first day's proceedings.

"To the day when we will be rid of the concepts of capitalism and socialism," he said. "Who needs these systems and their differences, when, if they keep fighting, there will be no earth, no life?"[17]

Gleb Panfilov

No Crossing Under Fire/ There Is No Ford in Fire (1968)
The Beginning/ The Start/ The Debut (1970)
May I Have the Floor/ I Want to Speak (1973) (banned—
    released in 1976)
Theme (1979) (banned—released in 1986)
Valentina (1981)
Vassa (1983)
Mother (1990)

Gleb Panfilov, together with such directors as the social realist Vadim Abdrashitov, the psychological realist Andrei Smirnov, the satirist and realist Elem Klimov, and the versatile Sergei Soloviev comprise an aesthetic caucus within contemporary U.S.S.R. film. While adhering to the structural conventions of traditional Soviet cinematography, these reformist directors have turned the content upside down. They stand in contrast to the aesthetic avant-garde, the art-for-art's-sake iconoclasts Sergei Paradjanov, Alexander Sokurov, and Andrei Tarkovsky, who sought to shatter all the norms. Paradjanov, Sokurov and Tarkovsky became official pariahs. Paradjanov went to jail for contrived charges of currency speculation, homosexuality and "incitement to suicide." Sokurov made some 20 films, but many went to the deep freeze, and he remained an "unmentionable" who is to this day unlisted in the *Kino* encyclopedia. Tarkovsky left the country and died in Paris. That is not to say that the reformists were without their own problems with the censors. Klimov's and Smirnov's works were frequently banned and two of Panfilov's most important films—*Theme* and *May I Have the Floor*—met the same fate. Yet it is the reformists who today comprise the mainstream of the glasnost cinema and the central leadership for perestroika in the industry.

The genre of cinematic introspection, which is discussed at some length in Chapter 3 with reference to Panfilov's *Theme*, is the director's forte. The heroes and heroines he chooses to portray are typically bright, talented, exceptional people whose inner beings are out of pace with their social reality. Even with his classic re-creations such as *Vassa*, based on the father of socialist realism Maxim Gorky's 1910 play *Vassa Zheleznova*, he brings a fresh perspective to the conventional aesthetic. In Panfilov's film version, the avaricious capitalist heroine of the work assumes human dimensions. It is the heroine's strength and her perseverance in the face of momentous pre-revolutionary social change and family tragedy that are emphasized in Inna Churikova's portrayal of the character. Panfilov's Vassa is more than a stereotyped representative of the wealthy merchant class; she has her own inner dilemmas, and her own unfulfilled potentialities. The victimizer here is shown as the victim.

Panfilov has most recently completed yet another cinematic version of Gorky's 1905 novel *Mother*. It is the third such adaptation in Soviet film history. *Mother* was held high by Stalin and by socialist-realist theorists as a model that all writers should attempt to emulate. The narrative master Vsevolod Pudovkin's 1926 film of the work departed from Gorky's original by integrating the real events of the 1905-1906 Tver worker's strike into the plot, and was elaborated by his seamless montage and powerful visual images of the ice breakup on the Neva River.

"The revolution was as spring," Pudovkin once said. "And as mighty as the spring floods."

Mark Donskoy's '50s *Mother* was by contrast an exact, literalist interpretation. The revisionist Panfilov holding true to form once again focuses on the inner conflicts inherent in the Gorky masterpiece and develops them with his own fresh detail. In *Mother* the naive heroine, who trusts the Czarist authorities, unintentionally betrays her revolutionary son to the police. After his arrest, she joins a demonstration where she meets her death. Like Pudovkin's script, Panfilov's, initially titled *Outlaws*, reportedly borrows from historical data not used by the novelist—in this case, the records of the 1902 Sormovo Strike and the memoirs of Pyotr Zalomov, who was Gorky's prototype for his hero Pavel Vlasov. The turning point in the script, intriguingly, is Pavel's passionate dream of committing suicide. Such a dramaturgical twist would have been anathema to the traditions of socialist realism.

It is impossible to consider Panfilov's work without mention of his alliance with the great actress of screen and stage Inna Churikova. They launched their movie career together with the debut feature *No Crossing Under Fire*. Subsequently she married him, and has starred in all his other films. *No Crossing Under Fire*, set in the Civil War, initiated the theme that has fascinated Panfilov for two decades—the paradoxical yearnings of the human spirit, cast against the contradictory demands of the social context. From this viewpoint the film was a radical departure from the traditional treatment of the historico-revolutionary genre. Its focus, like that of Panfilov's later work *Theme*, was the moral dilemma of the artist. Tania Tyotkina, a young wartime nurse-in-training, discovers in herself a talent for painting. Her talent, however, is unfulfilled because of the exigencies of the time and her life is tragically cut short.

Tania Tyotkina was the first of Panfilov's unconventional worker-heroines, although it is Pasha Stroganova in *The Debut* who typifies this characterization. Pasha is a weaver in a provincial factory and a naive amateur actress. Quite by chance a visiting movie crew cast her in the role of Joan of Arc. She has to overcome their professional doubts and demeaning attitude toward her plebeian simplicity. Pasha, like the heroine she portrays, experiences a spiritual transformation and rises to vanquish her foes.

In *May I Have The Floor* the heroine Elizaveta Uvarova is an outspoken former worker who has become the mayor of the town. In the tradition of Kira Muratova's heroine Valentina in *Brief Encounters*, Elizaveta confronts incompetent officialdom. She is the multi-dimensional tough modern Soviet superwoman: wife, mother, and dedicated community leader all rolled into one. She treats social duty as a serious matter and accepts no compromises, but she does not lose her human sensitivity. Churikova, in the part, thus becomes the vehicle to express the collective conscience of contemporary womanhood. Neither the film's assault on the bureaucracy nor the realistic portrayal of the modern female found favor with the male-dominated Old Guard at Goskino. Censors kept the film under wraps for three years.

Panfilov's 1981 film *Valentina*, based on deceased post-Thaw playwright Alexander Vampilov's final opus *Last Summer in Chulimsk*, continues the theme of women's integrity. Disillusioned older women rise above bitterness to discover spiritual wisdom.

Another Panfilov work is a revisionist look at Shakespeare's *Hamlet*. Churikova stars as Gertrude, a role she played in his stage version at the Moscow Komsomol Theater in 1987. In Panfilov's *Hamlet* the Danish prince and the usurper King Claudius are the same age, which sharpens the moral contrast between them. Hamlet in a sense becomes Panfilov, surrounded by Philistines, "bearing the whips and scorns of the oppressor's wrong." [18]

Sergei Paradjanov

Andriesh (1955)
The First Lad (1958)
Ukrainian Rhapsody (1962)

Shadows of Our Forgotten Ancestors (1965)
The Color of Pomegranates (1969)
Legend of Suram Fortress (1984)
Ashik Kerib/ The Hoary Legends of the Caucasus (1988)
   (based on Mikhail Lermontov's poem *Demon* and
   short story *Ashik Kerib*)

Avant-garde director Sergei Paradjanov, who was born in Tiflis (Tbilisi) Georgia of Armenian parents in 1924, entered VGIK in 1946 and studied with the poetic Ukrainian nationalist director Igor Savchenko. After graduation, Paradjanov worked in obscurity at the Dovzhenko Studios in Kiev. Then, in 1965, his richly textured, color tableau *Shadows of Our Forgotten Ancestors* suddenly propelled him to international recognition. With *Shadows* critics abroad immediately applauded Paradjanov as an aesthetic innovator—an appropriate heir to the lyrical tradition of Alexander Dovzhenko, but at home the film was labelled as formalist, and its director was soon in trouble with Goskino. From 1965 to 1969 numerous proposed projects were blocked, including what for other filmmakers might have been an innocuous classical adaptation, a work based on the 19th century poet-painter-novelist Mikhail Lermontov. The Lermontov theme would have to wait for glasnost and Paradjanov's recent film *Ashik Kerib*.

In 1968, after returning to his native south, Paradjanov got Armenfilm to back his second innovative feature, *The Color of Pomegranates*. Goskino hacked 20 minutes from *Color*, released it only briefly in 1973, then shelved it for 13 years. Meanwhile Paradjanov was arraigned for homosexuality, currency speculation and counselling to commit suicide. The homosexuality charge stuck. He spent the next four years at hard labor. Following his release he faced another four year period of blocked projects, then was arrested again. Although the notorious director was acquitted, he would not work for yet another two years. Finally, in 1984, Gruziafilm Studios produced *The Legend of Suram Fortress*.

At one level Paradjanov's films appear to be little more than imagism, vividly beautiful, but slow-moving and self-indulgent re-creations of myth-like historical settings. At another level they are richly suggestive, cinematic frescos which reveal a complexity of contemporary and ancestral meaning.

Shadows of Our Forgotten Ancestors, based on a classical novel by Mikhail Kotsiubinsky, set in the 1860s Ukraine among the Hutsul tribesman of the Carpathian Mountains, is a romantic tragedy in the tradition of Romeo and Juliet—in this case Ivan and Marichka. Ivan's father is killed by Marichka's wealthy peasant father, yet despite the unfortunate family history, they fall in love. Marichka drowns rescuing a lamb from a river, but Ivan remains devoted to her. He marries another, but he finds no solace in their childless marriage and his wife Palagna, seeing that their union is doomed, turns to the sorcerer Yuko. In a tragic struggle Yuko kills Ivan. That's the plot, but the plot in Paradjanov's films is insignificant. The director plays havoc with conventional narrative structure: dialogue is suppressed, action is stylized, subtitles reminiscent of the silent cinema replace character and story development—visual and audial detail is everything.

The isolated Carpathian culture is symbolized here as a kind of agrarian utopia, much like Dovzhenko's *Earth*. The tribesmen sound warnings with their elongated mountain horns, the trembita. Their life is at once pantheistic, superstitious, and primitively Christian. The aural images—the funeral wails, the eerie echo of the trembita, the ritualistic prayers—haunt the viewer. The visuals and cinematography make us disturbingly aware of every camera movement. Paradjanov's visual gymnastics range from subtle sepia washes to swish pans and slow motion to shock effects. In one especially striking scene, when Ivan's father is felled by the wealthy man's axe, his blood in close–up spreads to almost fill the screen.

Throughout the film the affluent and colorful traditions of the peasants' lives, their clothing and jewelery, their feasts, rituals and celebrations are presented in brilliant embellishment. It was this latter characteristic of the film that perhaps got Paradjanov in more hot water than any other.

His idealization of the peasant life in Czarist times hardly matched the official party line. Yet to the contemporary viewer the shock of recognition could not be avoided. In 1965 the primitive aspects of life had not changed much. The people were still sheep herders and foresters, but by contrast the affluence that they had in Czarist times was gone. Authorities considered Paradjanov guilty of Ukrainian nationalism and his film was regarded as antagonistic to the egalitarian state ethos and to Soviet collectivization. The director champions culture rather than the state. He spits on progress and he puts his hope in collective spirituality. The characters he paints, like those visioned by the director Alexei Gherman, are atoms of history; their actions against its backdrop are insignificant. Time moves, but culture endures.

In *The Color of Pomegranates* Paradjanov turns to the culture of his own heritage. The film is a stylized biography of the 18th–century Armenian poet, troubador and cleric Sayat Nova, whose name in Armenian means literally King of Song. Nova, a carpet weaver's apprentice, was born Aruthin Sayadin. He rose to become the King's minstrel, an advisor to the court and ultimately the archbishop of Tbilisi. In 1795 the Persians slaughtered him on the steps of his cathedral when he refused to renounce his faith. *The Color of Pomegranates* in Paradjanov's characteristic style exudes an earthy sensuousness, which gives homage to the Christian traditions of his homeland.

Evocative images of the lamb, flocks of sheep, wool dyeing and carding are interwoven with surreal scenes of trotting stallions in quasi-mechanical dressage. The central image of the pomegranate, the classical fertility symbol, emerges repeatedly throughout the film. The movie opens with a shot of three pomegranates which appear to bleed. The juice oozes like blood to form the map of Armenia.

Unlike *Shadows of Our Forgotten Ancestors* where active camera movement helps to create the film's magic, *The Color of Pomegranates* is a cinematic still life set to music. The elements in the frame are as carefully placed as if they were icons in a sacristy; if they move, they do so with ritualistic precision. The camera's eye is neutral. The camera remains static.

Cinematic still life is also the approach of *The Legend of Suram Fortress*. Here the mythical past is Georgian. The way to the heart of the nation lies through the gates of Suram Fortress, the walls of which keep crumbling. According to a fortune–teller, if the fortress is not again to collapse before the onslaught of invaders, a beautiful, blue-eyed warrior must immure himself within the reconstructed walls. The film is structured like a medieval morality play. Legend–based films have tended, like their literary equivalents, to be linear folktales which stress an adventure theme and focus on the great deeds of their heroes caught in the struggle of good and evil. Paradjanov does something else.

In *The Legend of Suram Fortress* it is the fortress which is the protagonist. The characters here are cardboard figures. They are Jungian archetypes who act out through two generations the abandonment and reclamation of their faith. Durmishkhan, a slave of the un-named King, is set free and given a horse, but the king's soldiers set upon him and take it back. He becomes a wanderer, and then, befriended by a Moslem merchant, rises to wealth and marries on foreign soil. His son, Zurab, returns to Georgia to become the willing sacrifice who entombs himself within Suram's walls. One can only speculate on Paradjanov's choice of the entombment theme which followed so closely on the heels of his own fours years of incarceration, yet in a sense it mirrors his own experience with the state.

We have in this film all the elements we have come to recognize as Paradjovian. *Legend* is earthy, sensuous, and replays his familiar fertility theme. As the film opens, the people dump a cartload of eggs into the sand. They crush them with their feet to make bricks for Suram Fortress. The suggestive nationalist images are also there, but this should not be taken as national chauvinism on Paradjanov's part. His interest is intercultural. Durmishkhan is transformed from slave to wealthy man in a foreign land. His patron, the Moslem merchant, is reborn in Georgia as the piper Simon. Durmishkhan's son immolates himself for the fortress.

Taken individually or as an entirety, his films are dialogues between the various national peoples and are not in themselves confrontational. Nationalism in Paradjanov's work is but a manifestation of generic culture, be it Ukrainian, Armenian, Georgian, or—as it was to be in his projected film about the 19th–century symbolist painter, Mikhail Vrubel—Russian. The centerpiece of the Vrubel movie was to be the Russian artist's 1889 icon *The Visitation of the Holy Ghost to the Apostles*, which is housed in the newly restored St. Cyril's Cathedral in Kiev. St. Cyril brought the Cyrillic alphabet to the Slavic Orthodox peoples.

Nowhere is the director's universal perspective more obvious than in *The Legend of Suram Fortress*. The child Zurab is given a fascinating gift by his spiritual tutor, the piper Simon. The toy consists of miniature figurines of saints and gods from various religious mythologies threaded on a string. Here are St. Nino, who brought them Christianity; Amirani, who was called Prometheus by the ancient Greeks; The Queen of Georgia's Golden Age, Tamar; and Parnavaza, who introduced the Georgian alphabet. Had Paradjanov's setting been two centuries later, he might have included Marx. The dolls come to life as they dance on the string and be they mythological, historical, or folkloric, they are a part of the legend and the personality of the fortress. Myth thus attains a contemporaiety.

His last film, *Ashik Kerib*, based on the Mikhail Lermontov poem, *Demon*, and the romantic author's eponymous short story, *Ashik Kerib*, is the tale of a Caucasian prodigal son. Paradjanov died July 22, 1990, in the Armenian capital, Yerevan.

Vasili Pichul

Little Vera (1988)
Dark Nights on the Black Sea (1989)

Pichul, who was 28 when he made *Little Vera*, has started an independent production company called Podarok (Gift). Unlike Bykov's new youth studio, which is state-owned, Pichul's Podarok seeks not only creative but also financial (capitalist) success.

Although his immensely popular *Little Vera* has drawn more than 50 million viewers, he received only a standard fee of 15,000 rubles and promises of a bonus. By divorcing his next picture, *Dark Nights on the Black Sea*, from Goskino's distribution arm, Goskinoprokat, he could live or die at the box-office, but he chose to do so since 20 percent of the profit would go to Podarok. His entrepreneurial spirit, heartened by perestroika and the absence of censorship, proved fruitless. The melancholy documentary-style comedy about two star-crossed lovers, *Dark Nights,* bombed.

By all measures (artistic and financial) *Little Vera,* on the other hand, was the first full-fledged product of New Model Soviet Cinema. The film is caustically depressing. A large, polluted coastal city is the backdrop to this modern drama of alienation. The optimism of the Gorbachev era is offset by indifference in hellish working-class life. Even a simple plumbing problem can poison the people's empty lives; there is nothing for them to do and they feel helpless.

Tough little Vera (Little Faith) lives with her parents, but quits school and hangs out with a bad crowd. She meets a nice student, Sergei, becomes pregnant and invites him to live in their home. She is constantly bullied by her nagging mother and alcoholic father who loves her as much as her husband Sergei. Sergei is appalled at the parents' disinterest and lack of ideals. In a violent quarrel the drunken father stabs him. A hearing takes place. First, Vera testifies truthfully but is torn by her love for both men. At her mother's insistence that their breadwinner's (father's) life is at stake, she falsifies her testimony, thus betraying Sergei. Since her husband will not forgive her, she overdoses on pills and her brother, an aspiring young Moscow doctor, arrives to save her.

"I hate you," the brother screams. "I hate all of you!"

Pichul's realism suggests that confrontations like these are all too commonplace. Vera speaks for millions of Soviets when she laughs through her tears: "This is the happiest moment of my life, but I want to cry all the time." For the first time in Soviet cinema we see explicit sex on the screen, the eroticism of which is lost in the frustration of pathological love.

"For a long time people have lived trying not to see the world around them," says Pichul. "My film has angered and upset them and they ask: How could you show this? But I'm not from Mars or America ... I grew up in this system, am a product of it, a man from this country, and these are my reflections on it." [19]

Yuri Podnieks

The Mask (1975)
The White Season (1977)
Ten Minutes Older (1978)
Constellation of Sharpshooters/Sagittarius (1983)
Sysiphus Rolling the Stone (1985)

Is It Easy to Be Young?/
It Isn't Easy to Be Young (1986)

Latvian director Yuri Podnieks grew up with filmmaking. His father, Boris Podnieks, a mainstay of the Riga Studios for three decades, narrated, directed and scripted numerous films and was a master of the documentary. Shortly after graduation from the State Cinema Institute, Yuri went to work as a cameraman. He apprenticed with hard-hitting Latvian cinema journalist Valdis Krogis. At 24, working with veteran Latvian director and journalist Herz Frank, he shot his first full-length film, *Out of Bounds,* which is a revealing examination of juvenile delinquents who live in a correctional camp. A year later he was directing his own film, *Mask,* and this was quickly followed by *The White Season* and *Ten Minutes Older.*

It was, however, his 1983 documentary, *Constellation of Sharpshooters,* about the Lettish Riflemen, which brought him to prominence as a director of uncompromising honesty. Podnieks travelled the length and breadth of Latvia to film and interview the last surviving members of this elite revolutionary corps who were noted for their service to the Cheka, the 1920s precursor of the KGB. In the film a monument has been erected to them in Riga as heroes of the Bolshevik Revolution. Podnieks contrasts this social veneration of them with the reality of their lives. *Constellation* won him the Latvian Komsomol Prize and took top prize that year at the U.S.S.R. Film Festival in Tallin.

His 1986 quasi-documentary, *Is It Easy to be Young?,* is discussed in Chapter 1. Within a year of its release the film had already broken the million-viewer mark, a record for Soviet documentaries. The film is unusual for its innovation on the documentary form, and for its candor about Soviet youth and the dilemma of returning Afghan War veterans.

"Here we have our own Lost Generation," young Soviet film critic V. Matizen said at an SFU symposium reported in *Iskusstvo Kino* (Film Art) in April 1987. "All the time we were told those kind of characters existed only for foreign writers, for the Hemingways, the Remarques and the Dos Passoses, while we didn't have any problems. As you well know, for a long time, it seemed we didn't have any invalids either." [20] At a cinematic level, *Is It Easy to be Young?* is remarkable as a film within a film. Podnieks integrates the subjective footage of a youthful filmmaker in the documentary. The surreal, amateur footage includes dream sequences, prophetic illusions and a startling concluding scene where Afghan vets, hippies and rockers wander on a waveless Ocean of Morality.

Eldar Ryazanov

Your Books (1953)
Sakhalin Island (1954)
Carnival Night (1956)
The Girl without an Address (1958)
The Man from Nowhere (1961)
A Hussar's Ballad (1962)
Bring the Complaints Book (1965)
Watch Out for Cars! (1966)
The Zigzag of Success (1968)
Old Thieves (1972)
The Unheard-of Adventures of Italians in Russia (1974)
    (Italian co-production)
An Irony of Fate/ Have a Pleasant Steambath (1975)
A Working Romance/ Romance at Work (1979)
Garage (1980)
Say a Word for the Poor Hussar (TV) *(1980)*
Station for Two (1983)
Forgotten Melody for a Lonely Flute (1987)
Dear Elena Sergeyevna (1988)

Eldar Ryazanov can be considered a senior citizen of contemporary cinema. He made his first film the year Stalin died. He studied briefly with the doyen of Soviet filmmakers, Sergei Eisenstein, and with the master of musical comedy Ivan Pyriev. Ryazanov has directed 18 films and simultaneously worked in theater and as a longtime host of the TV show *Kino Panorama*. Together with Georgi Danelia he now forms part of the nucleus of the Mosfilm self-financing creative group Rhythm. The group produced his work *Dear Elena Sergeyevna*. If Rhythm had created his first feature film, *Carnival Night*, or the first comedy of perestroika, *Forgotten Melody for a Lonely Flute*, it would have turned a handsome profit. Both were box office hits. Some of his films, such as the brutal satire *Garage*, however, fell into disfavor with Goskino and surfaced only briefly.

From the beginning Ryazanov loved to poke fun at bureaucrats and the privileged. Leonid Filimonov (Lenny), the cowardly yuppie second-in-command of the Central Leisure Time Department in *Forgotten Melody*, has a forefather in Ogurtsov, the sourpuss assistant manager of the House of Culture in *Carnival Night*, whose name in Russian means pickle. Nine of Ryazanov's last 11 films have been co-scripted with playwright/satirist Emile Braginsky, an association which began with

Beregis Avtomobilia! (Watch Out for Cars!) in 1966. The theater connection helped them evade censors. Stage and film versions of their works were released simultaneously. If Goskino objected, the theater authorities might not. If it could be seen on stage, then why not on the screen, and vice versa?

Beregis Avtomobilia rendered in English as *Watch Out for Cars* fails to reveal a Russian pun. *Beregis Avtomobilia* is not only a crosswalk warning to the pedestrian, it also has the ominous personal meaning "Watch Out for Your Car." The Robin-Hood-like hero of *Watch Out* may steal it. The automobile to him is an ill-gotten privilege, taken by the elite from the people. This citizen wants to even the score.

Of all Ryazanov's works none have ridiculed the bigwigs, indeed the entire social system, better than *Garage*. In this 1980 production, the Co-operative Apartment Committee For Elite Scientists, "Fauna," meets amid a shortage of accommodations for ordinary people, to allocate parking sites for those who have cars. Locked away from the prying eyes of the populace, they gather, due to a shortage of meeting space, in the absurdly appropriate, cave-like Museum of Extinct and Endangered Species where wall murals depict the dawning of the Human Age. First, the committee must determine the rules of order. The members bicker. They have all been promised a parking spot in the new garage, but there will be too few to go around.

The group is stymied until the herpologist (poison snake specialist) suggests something unheard of: "Let's do it democratically." The result is a predatory battle of Neanderthal dimensions as the backdrop comes to life and prehistoric sharks suspended by ceiling wires descend to provide a biting counterpoint to the contemporary cavemen. All agree that the Building Supply Commissioner's fur-coated wife—a notorious black marketeer— is the least deserving of a parking area. Then she arrives, and calmly reminds them that without her loans they would not have cars and without her husband's support the garage will not be built. Their premature attempt at *democratizatsia* provides no resolution until one exhausted member (Ryazanov himself) falls asleep behind the stuffed hippopotamus and the others unanimously vote him out.

In *Garage*, Ryazanov satirizes empty social promises—the ever-shining future—and the establishment which had always spoken glowingly of the great way ahead for the people, epitomized in this film by the garage project. In *Forgotten Melody for a Lonely Flute*, Lenny abandons his working class lover and his talent as a musician for his career. His greatest fear is that perestroika will displace him. In his fantasies he is reduced to playing flute for kopecks on street corners wearing a sign saying: "Help a Victim of Perestroika." Lida, his lover, brings him hot food and a policeman wants to charge him with vagrancy.

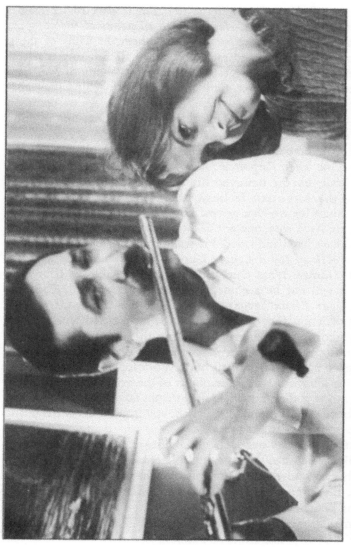

FORGOTTEN MELODY FOR A LONELY FLUTE: In this first comedy of perestroika, Lenny (left), the bureaucratic hero, abandons his working class lover, Lida (right), for his career. His greatest fear is that Gorbachev's restructuring will displace him and that he will be reduced to playing flute on streetcorners. (Photo: Courtesy Sovexportfilm)

The ironic musical counterpoint of the film is part of its magic. Lenny approves a generous one-way ticket to all points of the compass for the Tambov Choir, then he forgets about them. In fields of sheep and cattle, among primitive herdsmen, and on an aircraft carrier entertaining sailors they sing their suggestive theme song "Think of Me." But in the end, exhausted and broke, they are arrested for selling their costumes to pay for their return fare. "Think of Me" is the cry of common people to insensitive officialdom. Lida too wants only that Lenny think of her, that he love her, but Lenny has forgotten how.

"The film is a kind of parable in which the flute is a symbol," Ryazanov told me when *Forgotten Melody* premiered. "Filimonov used to be a musician, but he betrayed his art. The forgotten melody, or melodies are the forgotten feelings, the values like honesty, and respect—the things for which a person is born. But this man did not live his own life. He lived someone else's. He climbed the bureaucratic ladder. He could have lived and loved. He sold out to the highest bidder."

"*Forgotten Melody for a Lonely Flute* is a cross between my love comedies and *Garage*. It's a cruel film, but my next film will be even more cruel. It will not be a comedy," Ryazanov predicted. That was 1987, and *Dear Elena Sergeyevna* was in pre-production, but Ryazanov's prediction proved correct. *Dear Elena*, based on a play by Ludmila Razumovskaya, and written without the aid of Braginsky, is a dark look at the ruthlessly materialistic values of a group of Soviet youth. The gang at first attempt to butter-up a lonely spinster teacher by bringing her a birthday gift. The object of the exercise is to convince her to change their grades, but when the attempt fails, they terrorize her, rip the telephone from the wall, get drunk, vomit, hold her hostage and finally rape a young girl in her presence.

"It's a harsh analysis of our social difficulties and failures," Ryazanov said of the film which had the working title *Final Exam*. "The situation that the teacher encounters confronts most of the principles that she had taught them, the idealism of the Thaw, but today's pupils are cynical. The education system has failed them."[21]

His comments brought to mind that other failed product of the generation of the '60s, Abdrashitov's *Plumbum*.

Karen Shakhnazarov

Jazzmen (1983)
Messenger Boy (1986)
Zero City (1989)

Shakhnazarov's irreverent comedy of the generations,

Messenger Boy, immediately brought the young director international recognition. This film, which won top prize at the 15th Moscow International Film Festival, is explored extensively in Chapter 2.

Shakhnazarov is the artistic director of the New Model film association Start, which includes director Irakli Kvirikadze, *Messenger Boy* scriptwriter Alexander Borodyansky and Grigori Chukhrai's director son Pavel. Start has been set up as a democratic, but profit-oriented production unit which is designed to bypass the red-tape and frustration that have generally plagued directors seeking to make their first features. From the wide range of genres this group has explored in their first year of production, which include youth dramas, comedy, social satire, film monologue and contemporary history, it promises to be one of the most innovative of the New Model associations.

The bespectacled, puckish Shakhnazarov came to film with a background as a comedic short story writer. His sense of the kinky and the camp is revealed in his office decor which has one wall papered with portraits of Stalin in various sizes and another with images of Brezhnev; both are clips from his latest production *Zero City*. While no Soviet movies, or for that matter British ones, made it to the competition level at the 1989 Cannes Festival, *Zero City* was at least honored as the best of a poor crop by being shown as the closing film of the festival.

Eldar Shengelaya

Legend of the Icy Heart (1957)
Snow Tale (1960)
The White Caravan (1964)
Pages from the Past (1965)
An Unusual Exhibition (1969)
The Eccentrics (1974)
Stepmother Samanishvili (1978)
Blue Mountains or An Incredible Tale (1984)

Georgian Director Eldar Shengelaya, the elder of the two Shengelaya brothers, is the head of the Georgian division of the Soviet Filmmakers Union. Shengelaya graduated from VGIK in 1958 and studied with the comic and theatric master Sergei Yutkevich, who was one of the founders of FEKS (The Factory of Eccentric Actors), and one of the fathers of Soviet cinema whose film career spanned six decades from the era of the silent movie to contemporary made-for-TV flicks. The association with Sergei Yutkevich was a pregnant one and Shengelaya developed his own brand of unusual comedy.

Eldar Shengelaya's earliest works, *Legend of the Icy Heart* (1957) and

Snow Tale (1960), are co-directions of folktale re-creations made with director A.N. Sakharov, in which the pair blend folk motifs with contemporary images. *The White Caravan*, another co-direction—this time with Tamas Meliava—is a poetical story of life in a Georgian village. But with the 1965 production *Pages from the Past*, Eldar Shengelaya began to develop his own opus. *Pages from the Past* is a literary-based picture for which both Eldar Shengelaya and his brother Georgi Shengelaya were contributors. Eldar Shengelaya's portion is founded on the D.S. Kldiashvili's novella *Mikela* and is a unique poetic documentarization with a gentle life-confirming humor.

In 1969, Shengelaya filmed *The Unusual Exhibition*, an ironic tragicomedy about a provincial artist doomed to a life of making gravestones. The humor here, characteristic of the director, is critical yet compassionate, and possesses the typical Georgian moral undertone. Once the artist has compromised himself, his decision haunts him and returns its own hapless revenge. *The Eccentrics* explores another dimension of the artistic lifestyle. Here the focus is the daring and impudence of the artist. The 1978 film *Stepmother Samanishvili* confronts the life of the pre-revolutionary petty nobility with a curious blend of wit, melancholy and drama.

Perhaps his best-known film in the West is the 1984 production *Blue Mountains or An Incredible Tale*, an outrageous, and as the subtitle suggests, "incredible" work of the absurd. The ridiculously mechanical routine of publishing-house workers is lampooned to the limit. An author with his manuscript entitled "The Blue Mountains" can do nothing to spark the interest of the editors, even when he warns them that the roof is about to come down over their heads. Eventually the building collapses, but the characters carry on oblivious to the reality around them.

The Shengelaya brothers grew up with Soviet cinema. Their father Nikolai was the director of the silent screen who created *Twenty-Six Commissars* and the classic *Elisso*. Nate Vachnadze, their mother, was a famous film actress. Although Eldar Shengelaya has not made a film since before the beginning of the glasnost era, he has been instrumental in perestroika within the Georgian cinema, is teaching in the Cinema Faculty at the Rustaveli Theatrical Institute and is one of the leading figures in attempting to develop opportunities for Georgian-U.S. co-productions. He is also active in government.

Georgi Shengelaya

Two Stories (1963)
Pages from the Past (1965)
He Didn't Want to Kill (1966)

Pirosmani (1970)
Melodies of the Veriisky District (1974)
Come to the Valley of Grapes (1977) (doc.)
The Girl with a Sewing Machine (1980)
Journey of a Young Composer (1985)

Georgian director Georgi Shengelaya shares with others of the southern school—Tengiz Abuladze and Sergei Paradjanov—poetic imagery and limited dialogue. He completed VGIK in 1963 after studying at the Dovzhenko workshop and with Mikhail Romm.

Two Stories, based on G.M. Rcheulishvili's novella *Alaverdoba*, was his graduation film. The curious religious underpinnings of the movie established a theme which Shengelaya has maintained—the existential paradox of humanity. Hill tribes of all nationalities, Chechens, Lezgins and Osetians, all of Moslem faith, converge on the ancient Christian church of Alaverda for the harvest festival. They slaughter cattle, dance, drink and march in processions. The paradoxical contrast between these quasi-pagan rituals and the solemnity of the Christian festival are observed by an incredulous photojournalist. The tribal people on the other hand are as contemptuous of the journalist's craft as he is of their orgies. Following *Two Stories* Georgi Shengelaya made another adaptation, *He Didn't Want to Kill*, from the Georgian novel *The Reward*, and was a contributor like his brother Eldar Shengelaya to *Pages from the Past*.

His breakthrough came with *Pirosmani*, a cinematic reconstruction of the world of Georgian folk painter Niko Pirosmanishvili (1863-1918). Drawing on the painter's images and old photographs, Shengelaya re-created the artist's environment: Tbilisi's winding streets, the buildings, and the landscapes. As with other films of the southern school, especially those of Paradjanov, it is the backdrop, not the meager plot about the poverty-stricken artist, which is the most important focus.

The camera rarely moves and the shot length is extended beyond the normal cinematic conventions as if to simulate what must have been Pirosmanishvili's own intense view of life. At the same time the artist is shown only in long and medium shots, never in close-up. Thus he blends with the background. The artist and his cultural existence are one. Pirosmanishvili is cast as a naive Christ figure. Like Christ, his culture fails to appreciate him and abandons him, but finally venerates his spirit as its own. We see Pirosmanishvili's broad mural portraying the entire town where he lived, and then with an ironic and immediate twist, his comrades confine him in a cellar. His death is a re-enactment of the Easter ritual. From his tomb-like hovel beneath the staircase, he is called forth. His spirit, his art is resurrected.

The documentary *Come to the Valley of Grapes* continued Shengelaya's theme of traditional people at odds with contemporary society, whereas his next two features are forays into the musical genre. *Melodies of the Veriisky District*, the first Georgian musical film, is a series of eccentric and comical vignettes of old Tbilsi with all its social problems and colorful characters. *The Girl with the Sewing Machine* is similarly a musical comedy.

Journey of a Young Composer is set in Czarist Georgia and once again delves into the social paradox. In 1908, Nikusha, a young politically innocent composer, sets off an a trip to collect folk songs. The revolt of 1905-1907 has just been brutally suppressed, but the land still seethes with unrest and mistrust. When Nikusha appears, armed with a phonographic recorder and a letter of recommendation from his music tutor, both the people and the police leap to the conclusion that he is secretly plotting an insurrection. The protagonist and those he asks to help him in his musical quest get arrested. He escapes. The others are executed. The film approaches the surreal, when to fulfill their necessary body count, the Czarists snatch a passing peasant who takes Nikusha's place before the firing squad. Although the film made it past naive Goskino censors, native Georgian viewers saw it as an allegory for Stalinist and later police practices. Their perception was historically accurate. Until the period of extreme political repression immediately following the failed 1905 revolution, when police powers included summary execution, Czarist police would have exiled, rather than executed, political activists, except by special order of the Czar. It was for the Georgians, moreover, a double allegory. It was their art and their culture which became the true victims of the suppression.

Shengelaya's work-in-progress, *Hadji Murad*, waited some 25 years for approval from Goskino. The story involves a confrontation between Christians and fundamentalist Moslems that occurred over 100 years ago, when the religious and military leader Shamil waged war against the Russians. Based on Tolstoy's posthumously published story of the same name, the work is one which is perfect for the cinema. Tolstoy, after seeing the first motion pictures, told his tale in what he described as "the peep show manner."[22] The scenes shift continuously and the chapters simulate a magic-lantern slide show. It is no more surprising that *Hadji Murad* was rejected by Goskino in 1963 than that its original publication was also delayed. The conflict between the dominant state and the ethnic minority was as controversial at the turn of the century as it is today. The temporary relaxation of Czarist restrictions immediately before the First World War permitted the publication of Tolstoy's work. Glasnost similarly has at last permitted Shengelaya's. Alas, despite Goskino's go-ahead, the full cooperation of the Red Army for massive military scenes, and a multi-million dollar budget, his efforts to woo Western actors and co-producers for the film have proved fruitless.

Larisa Shepitko

Heat (1963)
Wings (1966)
The Homeland of Electricity (1967)
In the Thirteenth Hour (1968)
You and I (1972)
The Ascent (1977)
Farewell (posthumous, begun in 1979 and completed by Elem
    Klimov in 1981, first released in 1983)

Although Shepitko died tragically in a 1979 automobile accident, long before the era of perestroika, her work is seminal to the glasnost cinema. Like her husband, Elem Klimov, she was often out of favor and her work was frequently outlawed.

Shepitko graduated from the Dovzhenko-Romm Workshop at VGIK in 1963. In 1967 a long film consisting of four episodes by various directors and titled *The Beginning of an Unknown Era* was commissioned to mark the 50th anniversary of the October Revolution, but it was shelved before completion. Only a duology survives— her episode and director Andrei Smirnov's. A third was made but is lost.

Shepitko's piece, based on a story by suppressed Soviet writer Andrei Platonov, is titled *The Homeland of Electricity*. Faithful to Dovzhenko's primitivist lyrical '20s style, the film portrays the desperate hardships of backward, superstitious peasants and a young man's heroic attempt to pump water with a motorcycle engine to their drought-stricken fields. Despite their combined efforts, the Party-sanctioned scheme is doomed. Ironically, an illuminated star mounted over the village is the only visible sign of progress. *The Ascent*, Shepitko's best film, explores the world of POWs, deserters, collaborators and traitors. Her contentious theme, her psychological examination of moral issues and her overt Easter Passion symbolism confront official Soviet attitudes about WWII.

Farewell, her last picture, is about an environmental tragedy in a present-day village. It was completed by Klimov after her death. Her husband was also instrumental in saving it from the shelf. The film caught Gorbachev's attention, leading to promises of environmental reforms, and it is now a perestroika classic. *Farewell* and *Ascent* are

Shepitko's tribute to Russian religious values in which she sees her country's hope (Re: *Farewell*, see Chapter 1).

Andrei Smirnov

Hey, Somebody! (1963) (w/ Boris Yashin)
The Earth's Span (1964) (w/ Boris Yashin)
Angel (1967)
Byelorussian Station (1971)
Autumn/ Fall (1973) (banned, *Kino* lists as 1975)
By Faith and Truth (1980)

Smirnov was Larisa Shepitko's classmate at Romm's Workshop. They graduated together. *Byelorussian Station* is Smirnov's best-known film, a scrupulous psychological rendering of four front-line vets. *Autumn* is a romantic story of two 30-year-olds which was surprisingly shelved and *By Faith and Truth* describes a talented architect's difficulties with post-war reconstruction. All of the films show Smirnov's grasp of psychological situations.

Like Shepitko, he contributed to *The Beginning of an Unknown Era*. *Angel*, his boldest film, was the first episode, and the whole film was meant to re-create the expressive black and white filmmaking of the great Russian directors of the '20s. Smirnov not only proved himself up to the task of imitating earlier models, but like Shepitko in *The Homeland of Electricity*, he portrayed his subject with an objectivity that offended his sponsors. Moreover, he depicted it in a most violent way, adopting the narrative point of view technique called *ostranenie* (making reality strange) used by the suppressed '20s formalist writer, Yuri Olesha, on whose story *Angel* is based.

The dreaded, maniacal Angel and his counterrevolutionaries capture some Reds and civilians whose train was derailed. An intellectual who discards his glasses (so the Reds wouldn't shoot him) is set free. This is where humanity stops. Angel coldly lets his men rape a young girl and he caves in the Commissar's head with his hammer, muttering: "There's your hammer and your sickle!" Although Smirnov's film probes the individual psychological consciousness, it is also a metaphor for troubled times. There are no political distinctions in this seamlessly edited dark masterpiece, and were it not for glasnost, the film could never be seen.

Smirnov aggressively headed SFU, acting as Klimov's stand-in while the latter was busy on a new production based on Mikhail Bulgakov's novel *The Master and Margorita*. He proposed a structural re-alignment of the film system which met with a period of official silence prompting his remark: "Our cinema has changed, but just a little bit."[23]

Alexander Sokurov

Maria (1975)
A Lonely Human Voice/ A Solitary Human Voice /
The Lonely Voice of a Man (1978)
Sonata for Hitler (1979)
Dismissed (1980)
Viola Sonata/ Alto Sonata: Dmitri Shostakovich (1981)
     (co-directed w/Semyon Aranovich)
And Nothing Else/ And That's All/ Allies (1982) (doc. color)
Mournful Unconcern/ Sad Absence/ Anasthesia
     Dolorosa (1983)
Composition 15 (Evening Sacrifice and Greetings) (1984)
Elegia/ Elegy (1985) (doc. b/w)
Patience and Work/ Endurance and Effort (1985) (doc. color)
Empire Style (1987)
Moscow Elegy (1987)
Fireworks/ Salute (not dated) (20 min. doc. color,
     listed by *Soviet Film* M.7/87 p.16 as a 2-reel film)
Days of Eclipse (1988)

Sokurov is hailed as the new Tarkovsky; indeed, Tarkovsky anointed him as his heir. His career is not fully documented; for instance, there is no mention of him in the 1987 Soviet Film Encyclopedia *Kino* and like his mentor he ran into a bureaucratic wall. Both his documentaries and features are art films, and nearly all of them were shelved.

Born in 1951, he first worked in television in Gorky from 1969 to 1975. (This is the city in which the former dissident and post–glasnost member of the Supreme Soviet, the late scientist Andrei Sakharov, was exiled.) He completed VGIK in 1978, worked at Mosfilm's Debut Studio and later joined Lenfilm to become the leader of the new spiritual avant-garde.

Sokurov is a master of montage and shot all of his documentaries/newsreels himself, with the exception of his shelved film about the Normandy landings and the U.S.S.R.–Allied relationship *And Nothing Else.*

His early film, *A Lonely Human Voice*, based on banned vernacular realist/formalist Andrei Platonov's stories, shows erotic love from the point of view of a young man with spiritual pretensions who is at odds with nature.

Sokurov made several shorts about Russian culture and art, such as *Elegy*, a meditation on the great bass singer, Fyodor Chaliapin, who in the '20s went abroad on tour and never returned to Leningrad despite persistent coaxing.

Elegy opens with documentary shots of Chaliapin's re-burial in Moscow and cuts to lingering closeups of his daughters reminiscing in the singer's former house (now the Chaliapin Museum). There, newsreels and excerpts of his film *Don Quixote* are shown, accompanied by his recorded voice. Sounds and visuals mix to establish the link between a genius and his people, and the director searches for family resemblances, for any trace of the master's legacy. The daughters don't remember much, only Chaliapin's humor and thundering voice. They neither grieve nor condemn. And off the screen a voice merely sighs a regret: "Even geniuses make mistakes."

Fireworks salutes Bulgarian bass vocalist Boris Khristov. An overhead camera zooms in on a Leningrad crowd after a celebration. Cheers and gun salvos still ring in their ears as radios play pop hits. The crowd is blinded by the fireworks spectacle. Then a mysterious voice swells over them, higher and higher, and the camera moves upward to the stars. People raise their heads attempting to follow it. As the lone spirit soars, the color and resonance of earthly communal joy die away. A combination of documentary, visual and sound-recording styles interact in Sokurov's highly structured philosophical montage.

Patience and Work is yet another tribute to the talented—in this case young figure skaters. It explores what lies behind their brilliance. Leningrad prima ballerina Alla Osipova stars in this movie which is a mix of gossip–column exaggeration and newsreel, buoyed with the stylings of local jazzer Sergei Kuryokhin and rocker Boris Grebenshchikov. One provides rhythm and tempo, the other melody and mood. The film exudes warmth and chilly humor as the director cannot resist dunking Osipova into an ice hole.

Mournful Unconcern is Sokurov's first feature. It is based on George Bernard Shaw's satirical play *Heartbreak House* freely scripted by Yuri Arabov. If one is not a Sokurov buff, the film may seem contrived or pretentious, but it is a carefully montaged, layered and polyphonic fantasy, more absurd than Shaw's original. Three new characters are created by Arabov, one of whom is Shaw himself, appearing as a living "mask."

Shaw claimed *Heartbreak House* was a portrait of cultured, decadent Europe before the Great War and the motif of madness was inherent in his play. Sokurov intentionally exaggerates it to suit the sensibility of the Nuclear Age. Mr. Shotover's house becomes a latter–day Noah's Ark like Katherine Anne Porter's *Ship of Fools*, or Fellini's *And the Ship Sails On*. It is also a funeral barge where people walk about in kimonos, break into exotic dances, and Shaw, who is sarcastically portrayed as a Biblical prophet, sleeps next to Balthazar, Mengen's pet pig. Bombs fall all around the oblivious occupants who practice quackery, hypnotism, Buddhism, animism, and ultimately the cannibalism which is implicit in Shaw's play.

In *Mournful Unconcern* Sokurov also employs elements of Edgar Allan Poe's story *The System of Dr. Tarr and Prof. Feather*, which is set in a madhouse adding a further farcical-sadistic twist. And into the eclectic scenario he integrates parts of Shaw's friend G.K. Chesterton's sketch *Rhapsody on a Pig*. The Fall of Babylon is re-created in the scene of Balthazar's Feast taken from Poe's story. Mengen chokes on a piece of pork (his pet) to the soundtrack of Walt Disney's *Three Little Pigs* while the others continue eating. Through this we recall Nebuchadnezzar, who after destroying the Temple of Jerusalem went insane and lived among the animals, thinking he was a bull; hence Mengel starts walking on stilts shod with pig's hoofs. Ellie tries to wake up her hypnotized husband with the Biblical words: Arise and Walk! Mengel walks, but like a somnambulistic child. And one recalls the Biblical image of Christ casting demons from the possessed man, which become swine and like the characters in Sokurov's movie drown in the sea.

The central symbol of *Mournful Unconcern* is the Ark (temple of civilization and modern culture's funeral barge). In the climactic scene the Ark is bombed from an airship and becomes a floating raft. Tragically, corpses are thrown overboard, the animals swim away, and the sinking survivors turn into beasts. Shaw, who has been thrown off earlier by Shotover, is picked up by a warship. Unlike his characters who think they are outside history, their creator is not.

Sokurov's intellectual film shows that civilized society is responsible for its own fall; the tragedy of history (like Russia's own) is prepared by people who consume culture as if it were pork. This tragic cannibalism is brought about by mass hypnosis, a loss of consciousness. The film is, on one level, an extravagant affectation and grotesque self-parody, but this is only an illusion. It cannot be swallowed like a piece of pork with unconcern, or without choking! Sokurov's once-shelved absurd tragicomedy is at present alien to Soviet audiences who are not yet accepting of such genres, and may be alien to Western viewers too, but it provides an antidote for complacent art.

Sokurov and other artists of his generation are eclectic activists, reclaiming the continuity of Russian culture broken by their leaders.

With this inheritance, they can address their nation confidently: Arise and Walk!

Sergei Soloviev

Family Happiness (1970)
Egor Bulychev and Others (1971)
The Stationmaster/ Postmaster (TV) *(1972)*
A Hundred Days after Childhood (1975)
Melodies of a White Night (1977)
The Rescuer (1980)
Heiress in a Direct Line (1982)
The Elect (1983)
Wild Pigeon (1986)
ASSA (1988)
Black Rose Stands for Sorrow —Red Rose Stands
  for Joy (1989)

At a plenary meeting of the SFU, director Soloviev fretted that only 800 people attended his premiere of *Wild Pigeon*. When he was shooting *ASSA* and needed 10,000 extras for an outdoor concert scene featuring Victor Tsoy's group Kino, the leader suggested tightening security because ten times that number would show up, and did. Soloviev insisted critics take note of the U.S.S.R.'s new rock phenomenon. As a result, the pre-release publicity surrounding *ASSA* was sensational, though audiences were puzzled by the film because the hype didn't match the content. *ASSA* was more than a rock musical. It was a multi-layered work with broad-ranging socio-political implications.

ASSA's cinematic style is a pluralistic new eclecticism incorporating a detective story, melodrama, rock counterculture, and an elaborate parody of the '70s and '80s. The detective story focuses on the shadowy figure Krymov who was the Al Capone of Brezhnev's day, Krymov's mafia and their relationship to the militia and the KGB. In the midst of mafiosa intrigue we have a melodramatic fatal love triangle featuring Krymov, as the aging lover; Alika, his young mistress; and rocker Bananan, played by counterculture star Sergei Bugaev. Bugaev's songs accompany Bananan's psychedelic dreams. Other counterculture features include an outdoor rock concert performance by the late Victor Tsoy, and a film score by Boris Grebenshchikov. Brezhnev's stagnant era is symbolized by the setting of the film—Yalta winter 1980—the year that Krymov was murdered by his lover.

Soloviev's black comic parody of the '70s and '80s is dedicated to the boredom, phantasmagoria and poetic dreams of this period of inertia, when virtually every facet of activity from economic and political corruption to lofty cultural endeavor settled underground. Soviet society is aptly pictured as a shrouded world inhabited by chameleons, colorful figures wearing paradoxical masks. Krymov is shady, but he is also remarkably erudite and is nicknamed Swan after Proust's hero. The virtuous Alika is a gangster's moll. The captain on their cruise ship is a bandit. Another hood works hand-in-glove with the KGB. Saccharin restaurant musicians are rockers in disguise. These phantoms are two-dimensional figures trapped in their Brezhnevian present, craving reverie, knowing their future is denied. In contrast to the Stalin years and to the Thaw, both of which seduced Soviet citizens with never-ending promises, Brezhnev's static continuum is an infinite twilight zone in which they are embalmed. Pavel Lebeshev's masterful photography wraps Soloviev's metaphor in a gentle shroud, a visual time-warp—the surreal world of Yalta's snow-covered palm trees—in which the paradoxical atmosphere and beauty of the era are mummified.

The Socialist Art Movement (Soc-Art), a school of non-conformist painting banned prior to perestroika, has had an enormous influence on glasnost cinema, including Soloviev's. Soc-Art parodies the look and style of Soviet kitsch, portraying parades, official slogans, party leaders, even police informers. Thus political irony becomes the antidote to socialist realism. In *ASSA* Soloviev's own blend of conceptual art and pop is personified in Brezhnev's Nixonesque dark-suited portrait which provides a gigantic backdrop to the police investigation into Krymov's murder. There is a sharp transition and the film climaxes in a glasnost rock-in that blows away the mistrust, the threats and persecution which targeted Bananan-like poet-intellectuals for years. The late Victor Tsoy's music, full of life and love, rushes in a torrent to fill the vacuum of the lost decades.

Soloviev, who heads up Mosfilm's division for new projects Krug (Circle), is exceptional among contemporary Soviet directors for films which combine a classical respect for suggestive depth in the script with bold and innovative content, and careful visual technique. His multiple talent as an artist reflects his early background as a scriptwriter and a maker of classical adaptations such as his debut work *Family Happiness*, based on the two Chekhov stories *The Proposal* and *From Nothing to Do*. His interest in youth films also began early in his career with his 1975 multi-award winning production *A Hundred Days after Childhood* about adolescents who leave their innocence behind to pursue their artistic callings. *The Rescuer* (1980) and *Heiress in a Direct Line* (1982) continue a similar theme and with *A Hundred Days* form a triptych on the initiation of the young to spiritual awareness. His 1986 feature *Wild*

Pigeon may be seen as an elaboration of this motif. (For *Wild Pigeon* see Chapter 3. For additional biographical information, interviews, etc., see Index.) Krug is a grouping of anti-Stalinist, '60s-rooted directors, hence its title Circle.

As a Krug member, Soloviev has completed the farcical tragedy *Black Rose Stands for Sadness, Red Rose Stands for Love*. A collection of youthful social malcontents inhabit one of the last communal flats in Moscow's Arbat Street. A 14-year-old millionaire schoolboy is married to a beautiful 20-year-old wife and is the father of a baby. That is the film's farcical side. The tragedy in this absurd motion picture is a social one. Stalin is shown with a bedpan and Beria is portrayed with similar disrespect, but it is they who stood on the reviewing stand on top of Lenin's mausoleum to receive the people's homage. Addressing his portrayal of the two, Soloviev told *Soviet Film*:

"It was we [who] marched past in our thousands, and shouted hurrah: it was we who put them there, not some fateful and mysterious force."[24]

Endnotes

1. The Age Of Perestroika

1. Based on a tape-recorded personal interview with Rezo Kveselava, scriptwriter, in Moscow, July 1987.

2. Yevtushenko, Yevgeni, "The Heirs of Stalin" (translated by George Reavey), *Halfway to the Moon*, eds. Patricia Blake and Max Hayward [London: Weidenfeld and Nicolson, 1964], p. 220.

3. *Istoria sovetskogo kino*, eds. Kh. Abul-Kasymova and S. Ginsberg, et al., Moscow: Isskustvo 1969. Vol. I: pp. 5-8.

4. Khrushchev, Nikita, "For a Close Link Between Literature and the Arts and the Life of the People," *Kommunist* magazine, No. 12 [Moscow: 1957]. (As quoted in Tertz, Abram, *On Socialist Realism* [New York: Random House, 1960], pp. 40-42.)

5. As reported in *Kino* (German Film), Soviet Cinema Special Issue, eds. Dorothea and Ronald Holloway [Berlin: 1987], p. 8.

6. Romm, Mikhail, *Besedy o kinorezhissure (Conversations about Film Directing)*, [Moscow: Soyuz kinematografistov, 1945], p. 264.

7. Ibid., p. 266.

8. Klimov, Elem, "On Perestroika in Film Production and Film Distribution in the Light of Decisions by the 27th Communist Party Congress and the 5th Soviet Filmmakers' Congress," *Iskusstvo kino (Film Art)*, No. 4, [Moscow: 1987], p. 21.

9. Ibid., p.6.

10. Plakhov, Andrei, a review of *Repentance*, *Soviet Film*, No 5. [Moscow: 1987], p. 9.

11. Voznesensky, Andrei, "Fire in the Architectural Institute" (translated by Stanley Kunitz) *Halfway to the Moon*, eds. Patricia Blake and Max Hayward [London: Weidenfeld and Nicolson, 1964], p. 44.

2. Youth in Turmoil

1. Ivanov, Alexander, "Glasnost Means Intelligentnost," *Moscow News Weekly*,

No. 23, [Moscow: 1987], p.10.

2. The Moscow newspaper *Komsomolskaya Pravda* printed the detailed story on July 3, 1987, and an abridged report was carried by Associated Press on July 4, 1987.

3. Klimov, Elem, speech taped at a press conference for guests attending the 15th International Film Festival in Moscow, July 1987.

4. Germanova, Irina, in a taped interview, Moscow, July 1987.

5. Ibid.

6. Ibid.

7. Ibid.

8. This film was the official Soviet competition entry at the 1987 International Film Festival in Moscow and won the second-place Special Prize.

9. Lucyk, Pyotr, VGIK Komsomol representative, in a taped interview, Moscow, July 1987.

10. Soloviev, Sergei, film director, in a taped interview, Moscow, July 1987.

11. Laius, Leida, film director, in a taped interview, Moscow, July 1987.

12. Ibid.

13. Ibid.

3. Odysseys in Inner Space

1. Soloviev, Sergei, in a taped interview, Moscow, July 1987.

2. Mayakovsky, Vladimir, "At the Top of My Voice" (trans. Max Hayward and George Reavy) *The Bedbug and Selected Poetry*, ed. Patricia Blake [London: Weidenfield and Nicolson, 1961], pp. 223-224.

3. Soloviev, Sergei, in a taped interview, Moscow, July 1987.

4. Ibid.

5. Chervinsky, Alexander, scriptwriter, in a taped interview, Moscow, July 1987.

6. In *Esenin, A Biography in Memoirs, Letters, and Documents*, ed. and trans. by Jesse Davis [Ann Arbor: Ardis, 1982], p. 229.

7. Gherman, Alexei, interview, videotaped and translated by American film scholar Donna Turkish Seifer, Moscow, 1987, from a series of structured interviews with 15 prominent Soviet film directors on current issues in cinema and the effect of perestroika on their lives and artistic work. (Unpublished)

8. Ibid.

4. Directors of Glasnost

1. Based on a tape-recorded personal interview with Rezo Kveselava in Moscow, July 1987.

2. As quoted in Chukhrai, Grigori, *Ballad of a Soldier*, eds. Lawrence C. Thompson, Willis Konick and Vladimir Gross [New York: Harcourt, Brace and World, 1966], p. ix.

3. Christie, Ian, "Kino Eye: Soviet Cinema from Stalin to Glasnost," *Program to the 1988 Festival of Festivals* presented by *Toronto Life* magazine [Toronto: 1980], p. 308.

4. According to Irina Germavo in a taped interview in Moscow, July 1987.

5. See Menashe, Louis, "Rasputin," *Film Quarterly*, Vol. XL, No. 1, Fall [Berkeley: 1986], p. 18.

6. See Mikhalkov–Konchalovsky, Andrei, *Kino (Entsiklopedicheskii slovar)*, ed. S. I. Yutkevich [Moscow: Sovetskaiia entsikiopediia, 1987].

7. Kvirikadze, Irakli, in a tape-recorded interview Moscow, July 1987.

8. Ibid.

9. Ibid.

10. Ibid.

11. Romm, Mikhail. *Izbrannye proizvedeniia (Selected Works* in 3 vols.), Vol. I [Moscow: 1980], p. 540.

12. As quoted in Island Pictures' promotional release on *Dark Eyes*, prepared for the film's U.S. opening, Fall 1987, p. 7.

13. Muratova, Kira, in a taped interview at the 6th Vancouver International Film Festival, Vancouver, Canada, October, 1987.

14. As quoted by Stone, Judy, "Soviet Director Bids Farewell to Censorship" (Datebook), *San Franscico Chronicle* [San Francisco: October 11, 1987], p.33.

15. Muratova, Kira, taped interview, Vancouver, Canada, October, 1987.

16. Troitsky, Artemy, *Back in the U.S.S.R. (Rock in Russia)* [Boston: Faber and Faber, 1987], p.13.

17. As quoted by Lardner, James, "A Reporter at Large," *The New Yorker* [New York: September 26, 1988], p. 87.

18. Shakespeare, William, *Hamlet*, Act III, sc. I, in *The Complete Works of Shakespeare*, [London: Spring Books, 1964], p. 960.

19. As cited by Felicity Barringer, "Glasnost in Wide Screen: Hush, Hush, Old Stalinist," *The New York Times* [New York: November 25, 1988], p. 1.

20. Matizen, V., from a roundtable discussion "Ot otchaianiia k nadezhde" (From Despair to Hope), *Iskusstvo kino* [Moscow: April, 1987], p. 37.

21. Ryazanov, Eldar, in a taped interview in Moscow, July 1987.

22. Mirsky, D.S. (Prince) *A History of Russian Literature*, ed. Francis J. Whitfield [New York: Random House, 1960], p. 320.

23. As cited by Felicity Barringer, "Glasnost in Wide Screen: Hush, Hush, Old Stalinist," *The New York Times* [New York: November 25, 1988], p. 6.

24. *Soviet Film*, No. 8, 1989, p. 36.

Index

Milton Keynes UK
Ingram Content Group UK Ltd.
UKHW020328150824
446933UK00001B/10

9 780292 727533